INSTRUCTIONAL AND CLASSROOM MANAGEMENT FOR MUSIC EDUCATORS

Margaret Dee Merrion

UNIVERSITY
PRESS OF
AMERICA

LANHAM • NEW YORK • LONDON

Copyright © 1982 by

University Press of America,™ Inc.

4720 Boston Way
Lanham, MD 20706

3 Henrietta Street
London WC2E 8LU England

Library of Congress Cataloging in Publication Data

Merrion, Margaret Dee.
   Instructional and classroom management for music
educators.

   Includes index and bibliographies.
   1. Music–Instruction and study. 2. Classroom
management. I. Title.
MT1.M45   780'.7'2   82–45018
ISBN 0–8191–2433–8   AACR2
ISBN 0–8191–2434–6 (pbk.)

To John and Sarah

Table of Contents

Preface

Because rehearsal and music class time is at a premium, music educators must work effectively and efficiently every class minute to maximize learning and minimize conflict in the classroom. Sometimes teachers inadvertently contribute to problems in the learning environment which lead to loss of instructional time, distraction and discipline problems. A careful investigation of the effective ingredients in successful teaching and learning is necessary.

Few music educators are fully aware of their instructional and managerial practices in their classrooms. Leadership styles, managerial concepts, discipline strategies and learning theories provide some insight into the task of instructional and classroom management procedures. Because instructional and classroom management are so closely correlated, one can expect that inadequate instructional management yields undesirable behavioral consequences.

This book has been written to assist music educators in a detailed examination of the purpose and consequence of what they do in their classrooms. It explores concepts, skills and research on the topic of learning and behavioral management. Though the music classroom may be a unique instructional setting, with the adaptations suggested it is possible for music educators to employ these strategies to improve their effectiveness and efficiency daily. When appropriate managerial skills are utilized, educators may more effectively teach; students may more successfully learn.

Chapter 1

Introductory Thoughts

As a beginning teacher I was told that discipline is nothing more than getting children to do what you want them to do. Perhaps discipline never has been defined more succinctly nor directly than this. Further, the task of discipline has probably never been more glibly conveyed than in this definition. Just what is the discipline task and why is there so much concern about it in the music classroom?

Thanks to research, we know more about the management of human behavior than before. Yet teachers appear to have more problems managing and coping within the classroom than ever. To what educational philosophies and practices should music teachers turn for help in establishing effective management strategies?

Some answers to these and other pressing problems within music classrooms will be explored in this book. A composite of research findings, managerial theories, educational psychology, affective and aesthetic objectives, plus practical common sense provide a framework from which classroom management practices may be formed. To assist the music specialist, specific ramifications of these findings will be made with reference to the music classroom.

Why is there a need for a specialized book concerning instructional and classroom management for music educators? A number of reasons exist. First, the uniqueness of musical objectives must be considered. Music education involves the sensitizing of one's feelings, attitudes and values. While knowledge and understandings are cognitively processed and psychomotor learnings of performance are practiced, there is a constant interplay between the self-concept and the musical experience. A special climate is necessary within the learning environment because affective outcomes are at the forefront of quality music programs. The educator, in efforts to manage the instructional and behavioral aspects of music learning, may utilize or ignore this unique interplay. Proper utilization and management of the instruction and classroom behavior contributes to an effective learning climate. Ignorance or mismanagement may create havoc.

Second, in teacher-preparation programs for music education majors, there exists little time to formally study the topic of teacher as the instructional and classroom manager. The curriculum is often over-crowded with the professional sequence courses, general requirements and the music courses which bring the total credit hours of the degree in excess of other sub-ject area majors. While there are a number of courses and inservice training classes growing on classroom management, there seems to be even less time to appor-tion for such purposes while on the job. A concise collection of selected ideas on the topic is needed to acquaint the beginning teacher and refresh the experi-enced teacher.

Finally, the necessity for such a text can be demonstrated in terms of numbers. Music educators generally encounter a larger percentage of the student body when compared to classroom teachers. Typically, a general music specialist will teach as many as four hundred children per week. The traditional classroom teacher may instruct the same twenty to twenty-five children per week. A secondary vocal or instrumental teacher has more students enrolled in performing groups than the geometry teacher has enrolled in class. Con-sequently, the need exists for a handbook which explores various concepts and strategies that may be helpful in understanding, predicting and controlling the variety of behaviors of the larger number of students.

On the topic of discipline and teaching there are two ideas which warrant immediate attention. First, one cannot discuss instruction or learning without reference to classroom behavior. Instruction affects classroom behavior; likewise, classroom behavior affects instruction and learning. Second, a good disci-plinarian is not necessarily a good teacher. Yet an effective instructor is always a good classroom manager. The interrelationships between discipline, learning and teaching need clarification. Educators, unfortunately, cannot separate teaching, learning and managing behavi-ors into discrete tasks. However, they must understand the purpose and consequence of their instructional approaches because they directly affect learning and behavioral outcomes.

Discipline, indeed, remains to function as an essential ingredient in the realm of classroom manage-ment strategies, but the choice of discipline is only one alternative in the array of managerial approaches that are available to educators. At this point it would be helpful to classify discipline as a necessary and desirable tool to maintaining social order. However, it is only one tool.

To more clearly understand some of the overt and subtle differences in the terms "discipline" and "teaching," some notions, definitions and feelings about discipline, instructional management and classroom management need clarification. It is curious to note that synonyms for the term "discipline" are "punish" or "teach." Immediately the negative and positive dimensions of discipline surface. While it is true that during the process of music education teachers engage in both types of discipline, rather than classifying teaching responsibilities in these polarities, it may be more descriptive to categorize educators' responsibilities as those of (1) managing the instruction, and (2) managing the learning behaviors of students. Attention to both of these managerial dimensions is necessary because learning behaviors cannot be isolated from classroom behaviors. Both must be considered equally within the educational context. It is possible to come to grips with these two aspects of one's teaching role and manage them simultaneously.

Thus the title of this book has been selected with a special intent. Managing the instructional and classroom behaviors of music students calls for more than a collection of gimmicks and devices for punishing or persuading students to keep them acting appropriately. Rather, as the title suggests, the scope of the text is to encompass the music educator's dual responsibility (and contractual obligation) to plan, teach and evaluate the learnings and learners in music classrooms.

It may seem somewhat novel to consider the music educator as a manager. Throughout this text the terms "teacher," "instructor," "educator," and "manager" will be used interchangeably. When one considers the enriched and enlarged responsibilities the teaching profession now fulfills it is easier to understand these multi-faceted dimensions of education from a managerial point of view. Readily a parallel may be recognized between instructional and managerial activities. Instructional management includes activities from the planning of quality musical experiences through the evaluation of the learner's musical growth. The various instructional activities, the educator's personal philosophy of music education and the specific instructional strategies all create an impact upon the learner's behavior. The correspondence of effective instructional management and desirable classroom behavior, then, is a strong one.

A brief comparison of the terms "discipline" and "management" further portrays another important distinction. The root of the word "discipline," discipulus, is Latin in origin. It connotes "learner or pupil" (Webster's New World Dictionary, p. 401). The definition indicates that discipline is a training which fosters self-control, character, orderliness and efficiency. Though the presence of such behavioral elements may be welcome within most classrooms, professional educators know that school boards hire them to maintain a disciplined environment and much more: namely, to carry out subject area instruction.

Educationally, the age of accountability is here to stay. Vociferous expectations of American parents have been firmly and clearly articulated during the seventies' "back to basics" movement. They perpetuate throughout the eighties. Parents express their concern regarding discipline which has been perceived as the number one problem in the schools for a number of years according to Gallup polls. To be sure, parents are critically assessing the instructional as well as behavioral events in classrooms. They are persistent in their demands for high quality instruction and well disciplined learning environments.

Instructional and classroom management are terms that more inclusively consider the responsibilities of music educators in schools today. The root of "manage" comes from the Italian word mano meaning "hand" (Webster's New World Dictionary, p. 859). With one's hand, one may direct, control and administer instruction. Instructional activities inherently include the learner's behavior. Thus, the music educator needs to manage the musical learnings and the behaviors which occur within the classroom environment. Regrettably, there are some music classrooms in which one of the two aspects of management is out of balance. Consider the dictator band director who is so concerned about proper behavior that evaluation of musical growth is assessed virtually in terms of well-disciplined behavior. Or envision the music appreciation teacher who is so wrapped up on the reverie of the romantic era that the students are frequently wrapped up in undesirable behaviors. Because of an over-emphasis in behavioral or instructional management, musical growth is negatively and directly affected.

The critical working relationship between instructional and behavioral activities in the music classroom must be recognized. They work in tandem. A more detailed examination of both types of management as they pertain to the music educator and music classroom will further develop the correlation and overlap between the two aspects.

Instructional management involves the preparation and delivery of the learning experience. The effective music educator comes to this facet of instructional planning with a secure understanding of the structure of music and the scope of the music program. The sequence of the learnings is then ordered with care to bring about the selected learning objectives. Specific lesson plans with short range goals are then constructed to insure the acquisition, retention and transfer of the learning. To carry out the learning events, the instructor approaches teaching using a variety of strategies, modes and techniques which constitute a distinct instructional style. Learning rates are assessed as instructional paces are adjusted. The evaluative criteria are pre-determined. Resources to enhance the educational experience are identified and incorporated where appropriate. A schedule of intermittent progress checks is formulated while a feedback system supplies diagnostic signals that learning has indeed occurred, that problems exist, that review if necessary, or that pacing is inappropriate. These are but a few of the specific facets of instructional management.

Some of these facets are learned and practiced during teacher preparation. However, most teachers refine their instructional management skills with grass-root experience in their field work because methods courses largely explore these teaching skills without reference to the unpredictability of learner's behavior. Another limitation of methods courses is that they are often weighted in emphasizing the instructional management preparation to the exclusion of behavioral concerns. Though course work in instructional management during teacher preparation is absolutely essential, the development of classroom management theories and skills is equally important. For the effectiveness of instruction largely depends upon the effectiveness of classroom management.

Classroom management (or behavioral management) concerns the channeling of the behaviors and activities of the human resources in the learning situation. The classroom manager motivates, energizes, focuses and sustains behaviors on the educational task. For example, if the behavioral objective is to identify the voice types within an operatic selection, then the classroom manager must arrange the environment and channel the behaviors and activities to make the learning event possible. Behaviors which conflict with the objective, i.e. off-task behaviors, must be diagnosed, refocused and continuously monitored by the teacher-manager.

Diagnosis of what is occurring among learners in terms of learning and behavior is often painful to the music educator. Off-task behaviors, ineffective instructional strategies or a combination of both may be symptomatic of procedures directly contributed by the instructor. Other contributing factors may be within the limitations of the learning environment, poor scheduling practices, inadequate or inappropriate instructional planning and occasionally a composite of these factors. Since some of the causes of ineffective learning and disruptive classroom behavior are in direct control of the music educator, these factors are worthy of attention. They may be strategically manipulated.

Behavioral or instructional problems rarely are credited to one exclusive cause. Yet some teachers are quick to exempt themselves from being part of the problem. To be sure, teachers must recognize that the management of instruction and learner behaviors is a complex endeavor. It requires holistic thinking to track and coordinate both of the management tasks simultaneously. Whatever (or whoever) causes dysfunction within the classroom must be analyzed objectively and subjectively. Recognizing the interrelationships between the success of learning and quality of behavioral climate rests upon astute observations plus personal assessment of teacher influence upon the situation.

Effective teachers are concerned with the class-room management phase of their professional role because they know that a positively disciplined learning situation permits educational efficiency. Not only is discipline necessary for productivity but for social order. The preparation for and maintenance of a positive classroom climate serve the instructional and behavioral outcomes of the class.

Frequently the following is heard: "I cannot do anything to improve my poor situation because the principal won't support me" or "I have no support from parents; they don't care about music." These comments present situational problems about which the music educator can do virtually nothing. However, teachers can take charge of their classrooms and direct the music education program in an effective manner despite the most trying circumstances. Once the instructional and classroom management theories are recognized, the crux of the matter lies within the management skill development of the teacher. In spite of the lack of cooperation or the limitations of the situation, many teachers have tackled the managerial tasks effectively and on their own.

Proof of this point can be found in school music programs where all of the support systems are viable. The district may demonstrate strong backing for music in the curriculum. The parents' interest may be clearly visible in their financial and time commitment to the music program. The administration gives the music program a high profile in staff and budgetary considerations. All of the seemingly important ingredients of a quality music program are there. Yet, an inadequate music educator stifles the growth of music among the students. In short, the program is essentially a weak one due to the incompetent music instructor.

Obviously the presence of support systems that further the excellence of a music program are of precious value to a well-managed program. The point is, however, that their absence is not the sole cause of poor music education. It must be remembered that support systems function in an ancillary fashion. They can only support a quality program. They, alone, cannot create a quality program.

Organization of the Book

Throughout the five chapters of this book a number of instructional and behavioral concepts and strategies are explored. The first chapter presents introductory ideas on the managerial tasks that concern music educators. It presents a rationale explaining the need for a special book about instructional and classroom management expressly for music educators. An important distinction is made between disciplinary and managerial functions of the teacher. However, due to some overlap and interrelationship, discipline and classroom management are not perceived as discreet entities. The importance of effective instructional and classroom management is asserted.

Chapter two concerns the process of music education. The unique relationship between the aesthetic goals of music and the objectives of behavioral management is analyzed. The learning domains and the scope of musical activities involved in the process of music education are arranged within a model. Finally, common denominator behaviors are identified within the process of music education and the attainment of desirable behaviors in the music classroom.

Introduced in chapter three are preventive management concepts of two types: instructional planning and classroom organizational settings. The key element in this phase of management is planning. A variety of planning considerations is explored. Specific applications of these planning concepts are made concrete for music educators with typical classroom or rehearsal exemplars. Several research findings, theories of behavior and managerial ideas are interpreted with reference to instructional and classroom management practices. The research references verify that proper utilization of preventive measures serves to reduce, if not eliminate, many undesirable classroom events.

The fourth chapter imparts specific strategies to manage and maintain productive learning behaviors. These techniques may be incorporated within classroom teaching. These strategies strive to increase the effectiveness and efficiency of the learning process. Characteristics of effective educators are examined within the chapter. Illustrations of these attributes are discussed within a practical music teaching context.

Further research and literature on managing inappropriate behaviors of both individuals and groups are presented.

"Managerial Thoughts: Good News and Bad News" sum up the topic in the final chapter. With greater insight, a second look at the significant aspects of instructional and classroom management is taken. Despite the probability of conflict occurring in all classrooms at one time or another, specific self-help ideas are proposed. Educators, aware that they are able to manage the behaviors of students only to a certain extent, need not be debilitated. Rather, music educators who have keenly examined:

1. their philosophical orientation toward students,
2. the process of affective education,
3. the critical interplay between instructional and behavioral events within their music classes, and
4. the integral role of management theories in the dynamics of classroom groups

are able to secure and maintain a more effective teaching and learning situation. The students are able to learn because the educator is able to teach.

Contemporary writers suggest that those who are unable to cope with discipline problems constitute the majority of "teacher burnout." Uniformally the consensus is that children are more difficult to handle today than ever before. Thus, it is incumbent upon music educators to develop a positive, working approach to the management of music instruction and student behaviors. As music educators sharpen their skills and strategies in dealing successfully with learning and learners within their classrooms, they anticipate and recognize conflict. They learn to plan more preventively and effectively. They diagnose conflict situations. Their resolutions are more professional and satisfying. This, essentially, is the intended outcome of skillful management.

At the close of each chapter, several questions are posed for the reader to ponder. Serious meditation and thoughtful reflection will function as a catalyst to awareness, growth and understanding of the music educator as the educational manager. The reader is invited to thoughtfully deliberate upon the questions and ruminate possible solutions.

Chapter 1

Questions

1. In your own words, what is discipline? What feelings are conjured up at the mention of the term?

2. How can the role of a music educator be understood in terms of an educational manager? What is managed?

3. What elements of the teaching situation are under the manager's control? Are there factors which the manager cannot control? If so, what are they?

4. What is the special alliance between instructional and classroom management? How can they have a cause-and-effect relationship?

5. How is it possible to plan instructional and behavioral events in lessons from one frame of reference, i.e. the same objective? Illustrate with an example.

6. Why is classroom management necessary?

7. Rank the following assets of a quality music program. Let #1 be the most valued or necessary element.

   more than adequate budget

   highly capable instructional and classroom manager

   eager, cooperative learners

   supportive administration

   lavishly equipped learning environment

8. In your opinion, where does the disciplinary buck stop? On your desk (music stand)? In the principal's office? In the student's home? Explain why.

9. Brainstorm all possible support systems to a music program. List ways in which these systems can be cultivated to strengthen or improve the program's progress.

References

Gallup, George H. The 13th annual Gallup poll of the
    public's attitudes towards public schools. <u>Phi
    Delta Kappan</u>, 1981, <u>63</u>, 33-47.

Madsen, Charles H., Jr. and Madsen, Clifford K.
    <u>Teaching/discipline</u>. Boston: Allyn and Bacon,
    Inc., 1970.

Pratt, Rosalie. "Methods classes go to school," <u>Music
    educators journal</u>. (Sept., 1981), Vol. 68, No. 1.

<u>The Merriam-Webster pocket dictionary of synonyms</u>. New
    York: G. and C. Merriam and Co., 1972.

<u>Webster's new world dictionary</u> (2nd ed.). New York:
    World Publishing Co., 1970.

Chapter 2

The Process of Music Education

What is known about the process of music education? How do learners attain musical concepts and skills? When are affective responses made in the process of music education? What is the relationship between musical growth and aesthetic growth? Answers to these questions can be found by carefully examining the process of music education and by understanding the "affective connection," i.e. a special linkage between the musical goals of aesthetic education and classroom behavioral objectives. In short, a unique alliance exists between what music educators desire their students to experience and how they want their students to channel their behaviors throughout the process of music learning.

Let us first examine high quality music experiences. They are affective in nature. The experiences have influence upon the learner's sensitivities, feelings and self-concept. Musical outcomes of this type have been established as the primary objective of aesthetic education. We can find evidence of contemporary music programs which identify aesthetic outcomes as the paramount goal of school music curricula. The Comprehensive Music Program, for example, charged music educators with the challenge of building a satisfying and personally rewarding relationship with music for every child in their classrooms. This challenge is an aesthetic one. It is much different from the instructional goal of music literacy or spring concert.

It is possible in each of the curricular offerings of the music program to affect directly the development of aesthetic growth of students. While students study various literature from a performance or nonperformance base, they can become more sensitive to the affective power of the musical experience. Their various percepts will form musical concepts. Their attitudes, interests and values will modify as they are exposed to a variety of quality music. Meanwhile, aesthetic growth is contributing to self-concept growth, i.e. what students feel or think about themselves. It is through this self-knowledge that learners come to understand and examine their attitudes, feelings, values and behaviors. The very acceptance and knowledge of self enables the learner to control behaviors. This is the essence of self-discipline.

Once learners are cognizant of the various behaviors in their repertory, they begin to evaluate and form preferences for some behaviors over others. Their choices depend upon their values and peer pressure to an extent. However, during the elementary and secondary experiences, values are constantly being reshaped and reevaluated as peer influence, home, society, school and other institutions make their impact on their self-concept. Since the school does have an important role in the formation of self-concept, attitudes and behaviors, the music educator may skillfully harness this opportunity to its fullest advantage through aesthetic learning and self-concept development within the music classroom.

Securing the "affective connection" within the process of music education is a strategic instructional and management tool. This is due to the fact that the development of the self-concept is a conditional one. Hermine H. Marshall presents the premise that in order to establish an atmosphere which will facilitate the learning process, a reciprocal interchange of trust and respect must exist between the teacher and students. "Before this type of reciprocal between teachers and students can be established, the groundwork must be laid with a hierarchy of attitudes. The most basic types of attitude undergirding mutual trust and respect are those towards one's self: self-awareness, self-understanding, self-esteem and self-acceptance" (p. 19).

A more specific application of aesthetic growth and its impact on behavior can be identified in the analysis of the process of general music education. Throughout the various music learnings offered to students, an invitation to engage in a spectrum of musical activities is extended throughout a general music class. For example, the musical activities in an elementary general music curriculum might include performance, literacy, listening, movement and expressive composition (See Table 1).

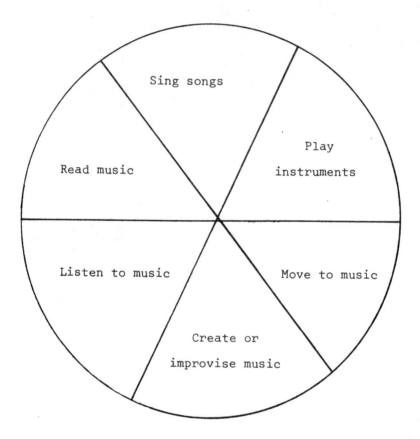

Table 1

Activities of the General Music Program

Through one or more of the musical activities within the program, students come to feel, know and perform music. They simultaneously form musical concepts which are accompanied by affective reactions: attitudes, interests, feelings and values. Because affective feelings, cognition and psychomotor elements are continually involved throughout the process, all three of the learning domains are operant during the learning process. In music education, the interaction of these learning processes creates yet another learning outcome, the aesthetic response.

Musical objectives may be arranged to incorporate a variety of learnings in each domain (The School Music Program: Description and Standards, p. 8). For example, within active music education, students process music of diverse media, cultures and ages. In the psychomotor domain, the performance of various literature will sharpen vocal or instrumental skills. Students may acquire knowledge and understandings of different types of music as they analyze and synthesize cognitively. Affective responses (appreciation, valuing and evaluating) will have an impact on the student's self-awareness, personal attitudes and feelings. As the experiences are evaluated, new musical values are formed. Meanwhile, the process of music education, when managed properly, may be structured to yield concommitantly the desired aesthetic outcomes with the appropriate behavioral responses.

Because most of the musical experiences encompass concurrent learnings in the cognitive, affective and psychomotor domains, it is critical for the music educator to attend to all types of learning in lesson planning, in addition to classroom behavioral considerations. If students are to feel the power of music affectively and respond in a sensitive manner with the shaping of feelings, attitudes and values, the cognitive and psychomotor learnings need to contribute to that affective behavioral objective as well. It is virtually impossible to accomplish an affective objective without reinforcement and support from other learning domains. The musical experiences do not occur as distinct entities. They overlap as illustrated in Table two. Affective attitudes accompany the rehearsal of every piece of literature. Concept formation enters into the psychomotor performances of music as students reorganize perceptions and grow insightfully as to the

15

musical elements and their innerworkings throughout the music rehearsed. Therefore, to insure that musical experiences are incorporating all types of learning and accomplishing aesthetic goals, music educators need to consider the learning domains and their impact on learners' behaviors.

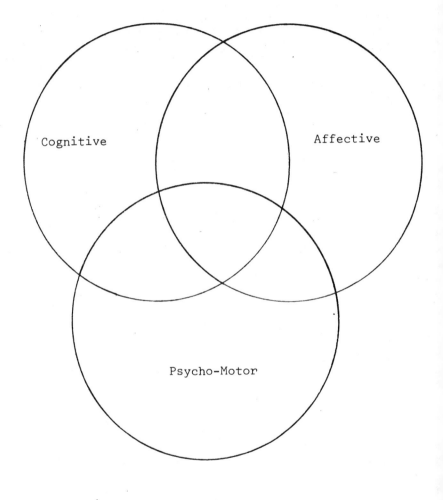

Cognitive

Affective

Psycho-Motor

Table 2

Three Domains of Learning

The process of music education has been described in some detail because educators often lose sight of the encompassing phases, overlapping elements and consequential effects on behavior. It is also necessary to review the process in its entirety to insure that the program's long range and short range objectives do, in effect, develop the intended designs. Planning a long term and short term nature, therefore, becomes a capital aspect of educational management. (A full discussion of planning is contained in chapter three.)

In Table 3 the entire process of general music education is presented.

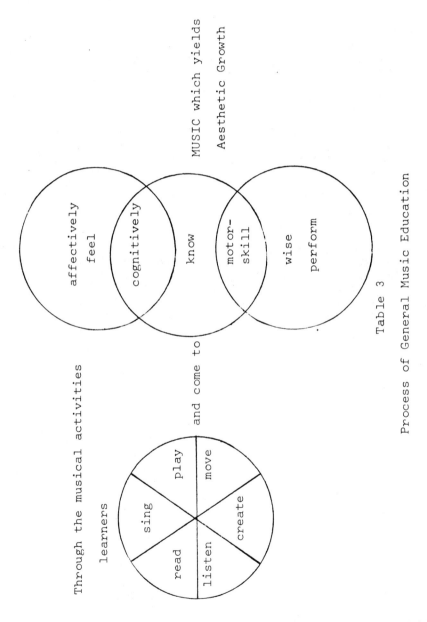

Table 3

Process of General Music Education

19

In summary, the field of music education appears to have a significant common denominator between its aesthetic goals and goals of behavioral management. The outcomes of these parallel goals may enhance one another. Hence, a simple deduction is made: linkage between the instructional and classroom management objectives in aesthetic education can be planned for and managed in a formative manner. The linkage is based on the premise that students must know themselves to be able to control themselves. It is possible for students to come to grips with their self-concepts in the form of attitudinal development, appreciation, acceptance of feelings and value formation through aesthetic education. This self-knowledge serves two functions: (1) in the fulfillment of the aesthetic objectives themselves, and (2) in the fulfillment of behavioral goals, i.e. appropriate responses to music education. As students gain insight within themselves they take more responsibility for their behavior. They are consequently more accountable to control their behaviors with directed purpose.

Music educators continually strive to affect the aesthetic behaviors of their students through quality musical experiences. With the knowledge of the special "affective connection" teachers may be able to manage the instruction and behaviors simultaneously in a more cogent fashion.

Chapter 2

Questions

1. Discuss how the linkage between instructional and behavioral events can function with the music classroom.

2. What is your philosophy of music education? What is the focal purpose of music in the education of youngsters?

3. Can a student's self-concept limit or escalate the degree of musical growth? If so, illustrate with an example.

4. How can one student's self-concept affect classroom climate and behavior? How can one student's self-concept affect group behavior? Illustrate with examples.

5. After choosing a specific musical activity, identify the cognitive, psychomotor and affective elements in the learning process. State the desired aesthetic outcome.

6. In each of these scenarios the teacher has made an instructional error. Discuss the impact of the learning domains upon each other in the following hypothetical situations:

   a. A number of high school band students have a negative attitude toward a contemporary composition which they sight read. What are the cognitive and psychomotor problems?
   b. The new vocal director presented a choral selection which had vocal range demands beyond the choir's capacities. What are the affective and cognitive problems?
   c. The general music teacher has introduced the concept of motivic development to a second-grade class. The teacher has asked the students to improvise compositions making use of motivic treatment on Orff instruments. Cognitively, what results are to be expected? How will these results be manifested in the psychomotor performance?

7. Using the model presented on the process of general music education, formulate a model for the process of choral and instrumental music education.

References

Gary, Charles L. and Beth Landis. The comprehensive
    music program. reprint from Curriculum handbook.
    Washington, D.C., 1973: American Association of
    School Administrators, Chapter 9.

Marshall, Hermine H. Positive discipline and classroom
    interaction. Springfield, IL: Charles E. Thomas
    Publisher, 1972.

National Commission on Instruction and the National
    Council of State Supervisors of Music. The school
    music program: description and standards. Reston,
    VA: Music Educators National Conference, 1974.

Chapter 3

Instructional and Classroom Management Planning

Adah Peckenpaugh advocated development of the diagnostic skill of planning when he cited the advantage of being able to "recognize promptly the signs that may portend trouble" in the classroom. In a sense, the educator must be able to plan in a "mental chess" manner by projecting learning experiences for students. Planning involves the close examination of the purpose and consequence of classroom events. In the act of planning it is necessary to anticipate and to prepare for the expected, as well as the unexpected learning and behavioral events.

It has been suggested that the most important skill a manager can possess is that of proper diagnosis and follow-up decision-making (Frost). As the educational manager plans lessons, a significant amount of diagnostic and decision-making skill is requisite. Throughout the task of instructional planning, music educators make use of these skills in such decisions as repertory selection, activity sequence, pacing and evaluation. Educators employ decision-making skills daily as they decide what is to be learned and how it can best be approached instructionally. In their careful planning they attempt to prevent undesirable behaviors by anticipating possible problems, recognizing signs of conflict by accurate diagnosis and resolution procedures.

The goal of this chapter is to provide the educator with ample suggestions for instructional and behavioral planning within the music classroom. Through careful planning a number of specific elements in the teaching/learning situation can be controlled by the educator and channeled to work for the successful accomplishment of the lesson objectives. These considerations are discussed in six categories:

1. The planning of instruction
2. The planning of physical accommodations in the environment
3. The planning of organizational measures
4. The planning of student-behavioral expectations and standards
5. The planning of teacher-behavioral expectations and standards

6. Matching philosophy and practice within managerial style

In each of the six planning areas above, diagnosis of one's students and one's situation is imperative. These data form what are known as situational factors. Decisions may then be made more skillfully with the individual situational factors in focus.

The Planning of Instruction

There are five areas of content pertaining to the planning of instruction which are very important elements of instructional management. These include: goal setting, materials selection, sequencing (and pacing), thorough and alternate planning plus initiating activity planning.

Goal setting

All persons in a leadership situation have a vision as to where they will lead their followers and how they will lead their followers. Teaching is somewhat of a leadership vocation. Music educators lead the music education of their students. Each music educator should similarly have a vision as to what musical goals will be attained and how these goals will be accomplished.

Goal setting is a tremendously significant phase of management in the business world. In fact, there is a distinguished management school, Management by Objectives, which is stylistically based upon the process of goal setting. In educational circles goal setting has received popular attention in terms of instructional behavioral objectives. There are many other types of educational objectives, yet the intent of goal setting is essentially the same: to set an appropriate goal to insure control and direction while avoiding happenstance.

Music educators Leonhard and House outline the importance of examining broad program goals through specific instructional goals for each day's instruction. Music educators may examine school objectives and align their program goals to them. Course goals may similarly reflect the broad program designs, while individual instructional objectives will divergently accomplish general course aims.

25

Thus the hierarchy of goal setting may be visualized thusly:

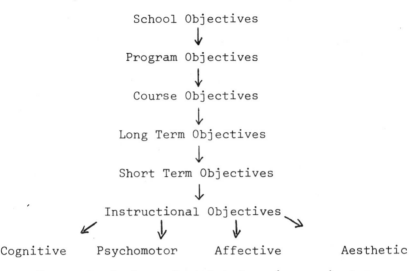

Many schools have formulated music curriculums which identify the long range and short range goals. However, it is easy to be short-sighted in planning procedures by being concerned about "what shall I do on Monday?" with no relationship to the long range goals. Long range desired outcomes are equally as important as short range objectives. They provide the educator with guidelines to maintain the focus and sequence of the "vision." Long range goals give each course a sense of direction. The scope of the study can then be detailed providing cyclical threads and continuity through the course.

Short term behavioral and instructional goals are useful in planning daily lessons. Cognitive, affective, behavioral, enabling, expressive and other types of objectives serve to accurately describe the specific type of learning intended. An excellent resource on the topic of musical objectives is Instructional Objectives in Music compiled by J. David Boyle. In this anthology, various authors reiterate the importance of objectives by exploring such topics as: the evolution of objectives, the formation and function of objectives in the curriculum, and the selection, implementation and evaluation of musical objectives. Instructions on how to write objectives and the use of objectives within state music guides, school district publications and other published resources is contained.

The importance of objectives is illustrated convincingly by Boyle in the preface. He points out that the arts are under close scrutiny as the cost of education escalates. He challenges music educators to demonstrate with a profile beyond that of performance, some accountability for musical growth, particularly in the nonperformance classes. One way in which an educator may showcase musical growth is in the process of writing, planning and evaluating observable music behaviors. Boyle reports that "the belief is becoming increasingly widespread that musical instruction often can be improved, and that the position of music education in the schools can be strengthened by formulating worthwhile educational objectives insofar as possible in behavioral terms and by providing objective evidence of attainment."

In addition to demonstrating accountability and improving the quality of instruction, goal setting has another function. For students to feel organized and focused in their learning, they must know the educational objectives of the music program. The goals should be communicated to all students so that they may comprehend the purposes of their learning activities. Many music educators overlook this important task. They fail to point out to their students why they are rehearsing a difficult rhythm or disjunct melodic leap. When students perceive the task's meaningfulness and purpose, they are more apt to comply successfully in the learning process and transfer the learning. For example, unless students understand the objective of a warmup exercise, they are likely to consider it a pastime, recognizing no relationship between the skill of the exercise and the applied skill in the repertory. Thus, in addition to formulating many types of musical goals, it is desirable to communicate these objectives to students clearly.

Materials selection

Another segment of instructional planning is that of selecting literature. When planning any musical experiences for students in class, chorus, band or orchestra, the first and foremost phase of planning is that of

27

selecting meaningful and attractive music for study
which achieves intended objectives. When the curriculum has been made meaningful, interesting and musically
worthwhile, dropouts seem to rejoin performing groups
or classroom instruction.

Mentioned in chapter two was the nature of affective learning which aesthetically invites the learner's
values to engage in growth. When quality music is
chosen for study, students have opportunities to grow
in value depth, breadth and tolerance through the
learning experience. An expansion of musical values
and taste is a coveted result of the affective involvement. The success of achieving this aesthetic objective
often is determined by the repertory's appeal to the
students.

However, an important note of caution needs to be
sounded regarding the "enjoyment criteria" in the selection of quality music. Educators need to consider the
long term results as well as the short term results in
their selection of music to be studied. Planning of
repertory in this mode is essential. For example, a
continuous diet of one style in the performing literature causing a predominance of similar affective experiences may soon disenchant, even bore, members of the
groups.

One might argue that teachers "can't please all of
the students all of the time." Indeed, teachers cannot
please all of the students and that is not their professional role. To be sure, the leader of music education is responsible for musical growth not entertainment.
It is possible to have musical experiences which students enjoy, but sheer enjoyment is not the sole cri-
terion for selection. Quality, stimulating music can be
chosen which is worthwhile for every learner to process.
Each musical style has excellent representative exemplars which artistically portray musical attributes of
the period whether it is from the Renaissance or rock
periods. Each musical style also has weak, unmusical
and trite exemplars that lack musical worth and aesthetic appeal. Often an educator's academic preparation
and performance experiences are limited in quantity and
quality of curriculum materials for particular performance groups. Such music educators are encouraged to
resume graduate work or attend professional conferences
which provide continued professional growth in this area.

The educator who selects and plans quality musical experiences that are strong in affective appeal helps insure on-task behavior. Boredom and distraction are less likely to occur when the instructional manager makes provisions for long term development of musical growth through music which is diverse in style, aesthetically appealing and progressively challenging. This aspect of planning requires thoughtful decision making.

Sequencing

The instructional task of sequencing is a fascinating managerial tool. There are two dimensions of sequencing which are distinct yet they contribute to each other's success. The first has to do with the acquisition of musical concepts, skills and sensitivities in terms of hierarchical levels from simple to complex, general to specific and concrete to abstract. The other dimension of sequencing refers to the actual ordering of teaching procedures that are selected to follow within a particular lesson or rehearsal and, thereby, create an instructional "flow."

To illustrate the distinction and overlap of these two types of sequencing, consider the following situations: In an elementary general music class the music educator acquaints the students with the concepts of beat and tempo before introducing ideas such as rubato, ritardando and accelerando. Students need a fundamental frame of reference in which they can place more specific, detailed concepts. An understanding of beat and its rate serves as the fundamental concept upon which tempo changes can be built.

Why does the choir director place warmups at the opening of the rehearsal? Why does the band director alternate between mastering tough sections in challenging literature and reviewing easier, well-rehearsed pieces? Why does the general music teacher order the various activities for the kindergarten class? The purposeful arrangement of musical experiences within the class period must be thoughtfully sequenced. Rehearsal or class time, when efficiently utilized, maximizes learning while insuring against frustration or boredom. The articulation of activities not only serves the acquisition of instructional goals, but also helps support a learning momentum with student behaviors on-task.

This tool is quite useful in managing classroom behaviors.

Just as the piano student acquires proficiency by way of an ordered pedagogy, it is necessary for the music educator to sequence skillfully the variety of classroom events. Unfortunately, learning is rarely happenstance. The planning skill of sequencing necessitates accurate diagnosis of the skill levels, the cognitive and physical abilities and consideration of the attention span of the students. The variety, duration and complexity of the activity are further sequence related decisions which must be determined in the planning of instructional and behavioral events.

Too often a music educator will begin a job in a community with little diagnostic planning. The music selected for the performing groups is too complex or too abstract. This has an immediate effect on student morale. Perhaps the educator could have consulted concert programs of the previous year. A quick inventory of the music library would further indicate past skill levels. Contacting private music teachers in the area may also provide background as to what students have achieved or are presently capable of achieving. All of these investigations may be done prior to meeting students. Meanwhile, the new music educator must prepare some type of lesson plan for the first day of school. These sources may assist in the diagnosis process. However, once students arrive, the first-hand diagnosis will supersede secondary sources.

Within each day's class, a further sequence of instruction may be planned. The individual period of instruction requires an attractive, stimulating and progressive package of learning activities. Ignorance of this facet of sequential planning very frequently causes misbehavior. For instance, it is very difficult for marginal listeners (ages five and six) to stay attentive during a twenty-minute listening lesson. In the instrumental program, all band students cannot meet the demands of forte playing during the entire rehearsal. Similarly, students may lack interest in a thirty-minute general music period during which they sing songs aimlessly one after another.

The purposeful arrangement of learning activities within the instruction period creates a "flow," if you will. If music educators structure learning experiences appropriately, the class members follow the instructional plan smoothly. Insensitivity to a balanced and well-paced activity schedule is an invitation to behavioral problems within the classroom. Rehearsals, especially, require careful planning to maintain a momentum of performance energy. Sequencing of music, sectionals and related activities is integral to the maintenance of high quality and efficient rehearsal.

Going a step further, beyond sequencing the music educator may plan to pace-check the instructional flow. "Pacing is the act of moving through each activity in a lesson plan in addition to the transition periods between activities." (Small, p. 31) The overt behaviors of the students will provide key information as to their attentiveness during the tempo of the lesson. Being temporally aware of how much time is spent in musical behaviors and non-musical behaviors often indicates pacing adjustment are necessary. Transitions from activity to activity need attention in the formulation of plans. Sequencing and pacing of activities and transitions are valuable management tools to the music educator.

Thorough and Alternate Planning

Thorough planning cannot be overestimated in importance. The music educator who is prepared to lead activities without wasting instructional time has prevented possible conflict in the classroom. "Running out" of things for students to do in class is a serious problem. In addition to the regrettable waste of contact time, students perceive the teacher as unprepared and disorganized. Generally, in regard to planning, it is advisable to overplan. Provisions for more than enough stimulating learning activities are most desirable.

Envision this scenario: It is Thursday afternoon, 1:50 p.m., and the music specialist is anxiously awaiting the arrival of the sixth-grade general music class. For two weeks they have been working on improvisation using syncopation, riffs, the blues scale and other jazz elements. They have listened to several instrumental and vocal jazz styles. A number of blues songs have been sung. In the previous class period the students began synthesizing the elements of the blues. They are now ready to improvise their own blues piece. Within their groups the students decided upon the instrumentation. Today's lesson will bring the unit to fruition with their compositions.

As soon as the students arrive the fire bell rings. When the drill is over they return to class. It is 2:05 p.m. A stray dog follows the students into the classroom. The students, naturally, find this quite amusing. Two students attempt to catch the dog and lead it outside. By the time the class is finally settled it is 2:10 p.m. and the specialist realizes that:

1. due to the two unplanned events, twenty minutes of instructional time has been lost,
2. the class now lacks the cohesiveness and focus for the planned composition task, and
3. there is not enough time to commence the activity. Fragmentation of the activity would be detrimental to its success.

What should the specialist do?

This scenario is not really that uncommon. Fire drills, accidents, immunizations, announcements, illness and sundry interruptions occur during classes on an occasional basis. The music educator needs to constantly entertain thought for "Plan B" (alternate plans) should "Plan A" (the original plans) not be appropriate.

Though the need for alternate planning was demonstrated in a turmoil situation, "Plan B" is functional in non-crises situations too. There are times that even with the most skillful planning the teacher makes judgment errors as to the duration of the activity. The educator may find that the students learned more rapidly or slowly than anticipated. Sometimes students travel off on valuable tangents which are unplanned but extremely pertinent and germane to the study. Thorough and alternate planning encompasses the likelihood of these situations.

How does one go about planning most thoroughly with provisions for alternate plans? The process begins during the brainstorming and consideration of (1) all possible learning activities and (2) all possible music to be learned. Some of these learnings will be deemed more suitable than others. Perhaps in the selection process of desirable activities or music, it is useful to have in mind materials or strategies which could serve as alternates or substitutes. As disgnostic skills are sharpened in the educator, the underestimation or overshooting expectations of student achievement and learning rate will decrease. But in the event of an inaccurate estimation in planning, a degree of instructional improvising is necessary. Certain plans must be readily available and substituted for those which were not effective.

Thorough consideration of the learning rates, styles and modes of students further demands alternate strategies in instructional approach. To illustrate, some music students are visual learners. They can read and make music from the printed page stimulus. Other learners are aurally dependent upon hearing the music before performing it. Various learning styles dictate different teaching strategies.

It is suggested that music educators maintain an "emergency file" of alternate activities, enrichment ideas, further resources and reinforcement plans which may "pinch hit" in these situations. The file provides coverage for situations which necessitate alternate approaches. Thorough and alternate planning also prevents lost instructional time while eliminating possible behavioral problems. To be sure, emergency file plans may enhance the topic of study in surprising ways. A sample of such items which may be appropriate for an emergency file is found in Annex A.

Initiating musical activity planning

What is there about certain days when the students seem to arrive in a "door-buster" fashion? Something special may be happening that day. The students, fully aware of the special event, look forward with great anticipation to the field trip, pep rally or other special happening. This anticipation can be true of the music period too. To what can students look forward?

Perhaps there is a musical riddle on the chalkboard for the students to solve hinting about the day's conceptual lesson. There could be a rhythm to read on an overhead transparency. Or the transparency may present

33

a mystery tune to be solved by reading the melodic nota-
tion. A new musical term may be reviewed through playing "hangman." Older students may appreciate a musical
joke, pun or riddle.

Having an opening task for students to do at the
outset of the period has a dual value. Instructionally, it may provide a musical challenge, review or
drill. Behaviorally, it channels student attention
and focuses it immediately on the musical task.

Opening musical activities have their place in
all types of music classrooms. Some music educators
of nonperformance classes find the "mini-quiz" strategy
a helpful one. The quiz typically reviews learnings
covered in the previous lesson. Students are permitted
to consult their notes or textbook to answer quiz questions. The reinforcement of accurate note taking, plus
the review of central information, assists in setting
the stage for the new lesson. Students enter class
knowing that the quiz papers will be collected within
the first three minutes of class. They immediately
engage in the musical task.

Clearly, immediate involvement in desired learning
tasks is worth the planning effort. In the performance
class the immediate task may be distribution of music,
the soaking of a reed or setup procedures which are
indigenous to the specific group. Students need to be
aware of the expected procedures as they arrive. Very
often getting off to a good start during the first few
minutes of the class determines the tenor of the remaining minutes. This launching device strategically ·
captivates instructional and behavioral energies.

Physical Accommodations in the Classroom

The physical aspects of the learning environment
can often be more powerful than the teacher in affecting learning and behavior. Certain situational factors
within the environment are within the manager's control; others are not. Those physical conditions which
warrant planning attention include: the sensory stimuli, the seating arrangements, the provisions for interactional space and the visual/instructional support
cues. Each of these planning areas may strategically
assist in assuring quality instruction and appropriate
behavior within the· music classroom.

Sensory stimuli

An attractive classroom has an adequate air system
and lighting treatment. Although it is not possible to
control outdoor temperatures, it is usually possible to
circulate and ventilate air indoors. Stale, stagnant
air may dampen the enthusiasm of students. Adequate
lighting should be insured for all areas of the classroom or the rehearsal facility. Teachers need to check
the visibility of information on chalkboards, screens
and music stands.

Of immense importance is the acoustical treatment
of the music room. Within the room the teacher may wish
to spot check to make certain that students can dis-
criminately listen to sounds. Because our art is of an
aural essence, proper volume and projection of sounds
must be secured within the room. Ignoring aural considerations within the rehearsal room may contribute to
undesirable sound effects throughout the class, i.e.
lack of sensitivity to balance, blend and expressive
qualities in the music. Other problems may also sur-
face--in the form of sound effects such as talking or
other distracting noises at inappropriate times!

Another stimulation is that of the olfactory sense.
Music educators need to be sensitive to this condition
within the classroom particularly after large numbers
of students have been rehearsing for extended periods
of time within a closed room. Often fresh air brings
renewed spirits in addition to a greater supply of
oxygen in the breathing air. In a sense, fresh air can
physically help to motivate learning.

Seating arrangements

It has been said that seating arrangements tell a
great deal about the teacher, reflecting the teacher's
beliefs regarding learning (DeBruyn). Where students
sit (or stand) often determines their type of behavior
too. Since the classroom manager is in complete control of this aspect of management, it behooves the educator to employ this tool to its fullest advantage.

Once teachers become more familiar with personali-
ties within their groups, they can arrange special seating plans which will modify behavior. In extreme cases
of behavioral disorder, it may be necessary to isolate

a student for "time-out" purposes. However, many undesirable behaviors can be prevented with a strategically planned seating chart. Quality instruction, even
within large groups, may be well delivered with skillful
attention to seating arrangements.

Using diagnostic skills the music educator may soon
sense certain personality clashes, rivals for group
leadership, positive and negative class leaders. By
skillfully placing certain students near others, or near
the instructor, it is possible to create a better classroom environment.

Unfortunately, there are no steadfast principles to
follow in formulating seating plans or furniture
arrangements. Further, as in the orchestra or band, the
director may have limited option in changing an indiv-
dual's position. Acoustic concerns may further limit
the flexibility of seating arrangements when a specific
balance is sought. Nonetheless, two factors need consideration. First, all students are unique. Their
seating patterns prompt specific, unique behaviors.
Whereas a certain location may modify one student's behavior, another student may find the same location more
conducive to inappropriate behavior. It depends upon
the various personality attributes of the individual
and peers within the location. Second, some seating
locations are prized more than others within the room.
So an area may function as the "hot seat" for one student and may cause reverse effects with a different student. Front row seats may be viewed as "neat" seats for
some learners while others may gravitate to seats in the
back row. Whenever possible, music educators should ·
rotate seats so that students do not become complacent
in one location.

How do seating or standing positions affect learning? Can students' participation level increase or
decrease due to their location? The quality and quantity of "musical life" around a student most assuredly
affects the individual student's output. For instance,
a student too close to a strong section leader may feel
"drowned out" and adjust to a lower participation level.
Yet another student may be motivated or challenged to
match the output and participate to a greater degree.

Rotation and experimentation are suggested to help
identify where the best location is for each student,

It would be unfortunate for any seating location to be perceived as the "naughty chair." The music educator may decide to locate a particularly distractable learner between two solid, on-task learners in the class. The likelihood for positive modeling increases in terms of behavior and learning. This strategy illustrates the critical importance of seating plans not only as instructionally sound but behaviorally beneficial. The seating contribution is a significant one to the establishment of healthy classroom climate. As seating plans are formulated the key issue to decide upon is the best placement for the best learning for each student.

Experimenting with particular seating patterns such as circles, semi-circles, horseshoe, rows or centers is recommended. Depending upon the objectives of the lesson, music educators may wish to utilize seating arrangements as a means of stimulating learning and discouraging conflict.

Provisions for interactional space

Another intriguing aspect affecting the dynamics of classroom groups is the furniture arrangement. Space has a great effect on the instructional interaction. Careful consideration should be given as to where the most strategic location for the piano, stereo, and other equipment may be. For instance, if the music specialist spends a significant portion of class time at the piano, the seating arrangement should complement that location. If not, the students may be comfortable and secure knowing the teacher will stay in that area rather regularly and that they can safely practice undesirable behaviors without being noticed.

Likewise, in the performance class, whether the music room is terraced or if the ensemble rehearses in the gymnasium, it is imperative that the instructor set up chairs and stands so that eye contact is possible with each member. The student needs to see and to be able to communicate with the director. Arrangements for this interactional space can be made through the arrangement of classroom furniture.

There is also another technique for making interactional space changes on a short term basis. These are referred to as the travel or movement patterns of the instructor. It is sometimes necessary to change the interactional space between two students who are clearly off-task in their behaviors. Or it may be necessary to close up the space between a student and the instructor. Directors who "walk through" their groups often hear musical surprises! For instance, within a large performing organization, it may be helpful to listen at close proximity to certain sections. Thus, planning changes in the interactional space of sections or individuals can serve as an effective instructional and behavioral management tool for the music educator.

Visual/instructional support cues

As for visual stimulation, what do students see upon entering the music room? If music is scattered around, if the floors are unkempt, if bulletin boards are bare or faded with age, if piano keys are dirty and the teacher's desk is disorganized, what impression have they? Preparation for students' arrival is quite evident in the visual stimuli presented the very first day of school. It seems that the initial atmosphere perceived by students is often the cue that they replicate in their attitude and behavior. Constructive visual aids, classroom orderliness and attractiveness teach by good example the proper care and use of learning equipment in the music program. It is possible to model the desirable climate from the first day of classes to inspire, teach and motivate students appropriately.

The visual cues within the classroom create a climate upon entering the room. The prepared music · educator utilizes this opportunity to model the appropriate respect for classroom materials and personal interactions.

Planning Organizational Measures

Organizational measures consist of several basic common-sense approaches which are often overlooked. These procedures must be planned because their impact upon the learning effectiveness is directly measurable. Since the procedures are often presumed, they tend to be taken for granted because of their simplicity. Thus, they are easily forgotten.

The organizational measures which are outlined

within this subheading of planning are classroom readiness, teacher consultation, leadership assignments and initial contact with parents. Planning and preparation in each of these categories may help alleviate some "first day jitters" and commence the school year with a good start.

Classroom readiness

When a classroom is ready for learners, learning may take place. This means that the furniture, materials and equipment are in appropriate locations in order to expedite the learning process smoothly. When not in use, materials should be stored properly. Current books or music may be stored in a ready-access location to avoid time loss in acquisition and distribution. Instruments require storage locations that provide protection from moisture and heat. Organization of instruments in storage units is a time-efficient strategy which allows students to locate quickly and return their instruments when not in use. Recordings, likewise, are more easily identified if they are carefully catalogued and stored. Audio-visual equipment should be secured and readily accessible for illustrative purposes prior to the time of actual use. Such organization, then, prevents time loss or confusion during the coveted instructional minutes.

The old adage that actions speak louder than words is true when it comes to modeling the treatment of equipment and instructional materials. The care with which teachers model during their handling of music, stands, instruments, books or recordings can easily be mirrored by students. This is particularly important for instrumental programs which lease instruments to students. Demonstrations of appropriate care for musical equipment and materials is a necessary component of each program in the music curriculum.

The organization and proper utilization of all learning resources and equipment may truly support the excellence of the program. These readiness measures function as preventive discipline strategies too. To illustrate, if the general music specialist has a back-to-back schedule with little, if any, time to regroup learning materials from class to class, this advance readiness will save lost minutes in locating books, records or other teaching tools. In these situations instructional time may be conserved and maximized for active learning--not passive waiting--as the teacher borrows instructional time for classroom readiness purposes. Unnecessary interruptions, pauses or delays are eliminated from the flow of the lesson. Students will be able to understand the organization and to feel the momentum of a well-planned lesson.

Classroom teacher consultation

For teachers, the greatest anticipation of the new school year is in the meeting of their students. Sometimes it is possible to have advance information on special students prior to their actual arrival. This knowledge may be obtained from academic files, through visiting with former teachers or consulting special teachers. Many educators argue that second-hand knowledge can often prescribe and dictate negative expectations on the part of the new teacher. But the concern here is strictly with knowledge about the best interests of the special child. There may be concrete difficulties, such as specific learning disabilities, for which the music educator must be aware and make adaptations accordingly.

Consider the physical disability of a student which may be more tactfully dealt with if the music educator is prepared. To illustrate, a student in a wheelchair may blend in more unobtrusively if the director has made provisions for the handicapped student's movement within the room. Special seating arrangements may be planned ahead of time to assure the best physical accommodations.

These and other adjustments can be articulated smoothly if the music educator has pertinent information prior to the student's arrival. For instance, the most grandiose of plans are thwarted if the educational manager has not accurate insight as to the gross and fine motor skills of students who are mainstreamed. Adjustments in the instructional planning can encompass the special needs, ability and skill levels in the activity schedule. This functional information regarding the special learner not only assists in the adjustment of the individual to the large group, but also in the adjustment of the large group to the special individual. It is clearly a two-way adjustment.

Finally, special classroom management plans can be

constructed a priori if the educator is aware of particular problems. Emotional disruptions, convulsions and other behavioral disorders can be more effectively managed if the teacher has knowledge of their possible occurrence. Much of this information may be learned by examining a student's file.

Some students, unfortunately, are victims of labeling in certain content areas. They are stigmatized with a label and with the low level of expectations. This sort of "type casting" has little validity in terms of musical ability expectations. Mainstreamed students grow in musical sensitivity along with every other student. The placement of ceilings on musical growth in such a fashion is highly questionable. Rather, the music educator may wish to learn what the student's physical, verbal, sensory and behavioral limitations are and devise a learning plan accordingly.

In summary, gaining knowledge about students who have special needs through the consultation with former teachers, counselor, nurses, resource teachers or files has a strategic place in the successful adjustment of a student academically and behaviorally. An informed teacher advantageously utilizes pertinent knowledge to assure a successful educational experience not only for the individual learner but for the entire class.

Leadership Assignments

Performing groups frequently have librarians or secretaries to distribute or organize music and folders. Similarly, general music specialists may employ helpers to distribute, maintain and collect learning materials or equipment. This may be referred to as the "captain" technique.

The captain technique is quite useful in generating a climate of classroom leadership and responsibility. Because a general music period may contain a number of diverse activities which require various learning tools, the captains may be assigned to distribute and collect books, instruments, papers, pencils, and so forth. Students in authority positions quickly learn responsibility and respect for classroom materials.

Though a secondary school performing group may utilize only one librarian per semester, typically the leadership assignment rotates in the elementary school. Throughout the interim of the school year, each general music student may have an internship during which the student is captain of something. On occasion it may be necessary to terminate a child's internship should the responsibility be ignored or abused. Generally, however, most students rise to the leadership role when the responsibility is presented properly.

Classroom leadership is an essential element to any group of students not only in terms of the extra sets of helping hands, but in the establishment of responsibilities for learning and behavior. The use of the captain technique provides meaningful experience for students at any age to exercise respect, responsibility and leadership. These are welcome, positive behaviors which enhance the classroom climate.

Initial Contact with Parents

Teachers have a powerful ally and information source in the parents or guardians of their students. Music educators may profit from a fringe-benefit relationship with many more parents than a typical classroom teacher. This is partially due to the fact that music educators frequently encounter more students in their programs. But, more so, they have students in their classes for several years continuously. In addition, music educators have opportunities under the most pleasant of circumstances to meet parents through the high profile of performance gatherings.

This special parental contact may be used profitably if the educator plans ahead and communicates clearly to parents what the expected behaviors are in the music program. Sowing these seeds of understanding and rapport early will lead to a better relationship with parents should it be necessary to contact them later regarding academic or behavioral concerns. Whether the music educator calls home to inform parents of exceedingly good progress or totally unacceptable behavior, the educator is on better footing if the expectations of the program have been communicated at the outset of the school year. (It is necessary to mention here that new music educators may wish to familiarize themselves with the "chain of command" when difficulties arise. In some schools it is protocol to refer specific concerns to the dean of discipline or counselor. Some administrators prefer to make the phone calls themselves. In any event, teachers should be acquainted with the procedures prior to acting on specific problems.)

Very often music educators only resort to contacting parents when there are serious problems to be reported. The placement of a positive "sunshine call," however, may be more powerful than the negative counterpart. For instance, if the music educator calls home to express appreciation for the support parents are contributing to the child's growth in terms of practicing, that student may model the desirable learning behaviors for others. Make no mistake, students talk to one another. Therefore, if it is known that the band director called a student's home with a praise message, it may cause a behavioral wonder: students may better realize the appropriate levels of academic work and behaviors. Further, they may be more motivated to meet these standards.

Planning ahead in the realm of public relations can be a winning strategy. To be sure, teachers need to keep mindful that most parents wish to be informed and up-to-date with the progress of their children. Expectations are best communicated early within the school year. Follow-up communication can then spring from the foundational contact.

Planning of Student Behavioral Expectations and Standards

Several authors have expressed the need to anticipate learning and behavioral problems. The premise that scrupulous and thorough planning of instructional activities and learning outcomes can directly affect the behavior of students is true. Therefore, along with the planning of long term instructional goals, music educators must consider their behavioral goals on a long term and daily basis. Once these goals are identified, their expectations can be formulated.

How does the classroom manager plan behavioral objectives in a preventive sense? Primarily the response to this query lies in the preparation of a two-fold plan:

1. Formulating and expressing behavioral expectations

2. Setting limits through the establishment of classroom rules.

From a behavioristic point of view, the teacher's actions in the classroom demonstrate the teacher's beliefs about learners and learning. In other words, how a teacher treats students reflects how the teacher feels or what the teacher believes about students. Undergirding philosophies, then, are actualized in one's classroom management practices.

There is an interesting managerial theory known as Theory X Theory Y. It is a classification of attitudes towards workers (or, in this case, students) which helps illustrate the broad spectrum of managerial styles in the classroom. Theory X educators perceive students as lazy, incompetent and untrustworthy individuals. It follows that certain strategies would carry out these beliefs and be reflected in the leadership style. The interpersonal relationships within the classroom would also be influenced by the Theory X orientation. In addition, a Theory X educator sets a distinctive motivational level. Students then respond to the leadership style, motivational level and quality of interpersonal relationships. To illustrate, there have been studies conducted by Lewin, Lippitt and White indicating that an autocratic leadership style promoted aggressive acts among groups of elementary school boys. Productivity and group behavior were directly affected by the Theory X disposition.

A Theory Y educator holds that students are industrious, competent and trusting learners. Clearly, the classroom management practices would differ according to the attitudinal disposition of the Theory Y teacher. The leadership style and interpersonal relationships within the classroom generate a different climate. In addition, the quality of motivation differs. Productivity and behavior results differ because of the basic Theory Y attitude toward learners.

The determining factor as to why certain behavioral management strategies are practiced over others is rooted in the attitudes the educator holds towards the learner. In fact, when conflict arises in the classroom, one author maintains that successful solutions to classroom problems begin only with the teacher's attitude (DeBruyn).

Though Theory X and Theory Y present two radically opposing attitudes towards learners, it is not difficult to find educators who lean towards the Theory X or Theory Y orientation. Most teachers, however, fall somewhere in between.

The Theory X and Theory Y construct of attitudes hints at expectancy theory. Expectancy theory includes the anticipated behaviors and achievements educators maintain for their students. The familiar Rosenthal studies manifesting the Pygmalion Effect in the classroom suggest that the quality of expectations educators set for their students often determines the quality of achievement. As teachers expect, so do student produce--occasionally regardless of ability level. Setting behavioral expectations for students is a most important task for music educators to undertake. The level of expectations for classroom behavior, in particular, can determine the type of classroom interaction. High, strong expectations for what is appropriate and desirable in the classroom must be understood by all students. For, if the expectations are low or even mediocre, the students will merely live up to second-rate levels. Music educators need to take into account the factor that expectations are operant for not only the entire school year but also for the ensuing years.

If expectations are not conveyed to students, they will continue to "test the teacher" to find the limits. This is due to the fact that students are not psychologically comfortable until they are aware of the limits of their freedom in the classroom. Lack of expectations creates a shotgun approach to classroom management consisting of continual reminders. The interesting issue in this situation is that some students really do not know how they should behave when expectations and standards have not been conveyed. It is, therefore, incumbent upon the educator to introduce these topics and assure their comprehension. Both expectations and limits must be constructed and clearly communicated to students, preferably at the outset of the school year.

In fact, the student participation in the limit or rule-setting process may be a meaningful endeavor. Depending upon the group of students, the music educator may wish to enlist the students cooperatively in the decision-making process. The joint responsibility of establishing and reinforcing a code of behavior may foster a degree of participative management. A climate of responsibility reflecting the composite of individual's contributions and cooperation is created. Research also confirms that a certain level of motivation to support group-decision results occurs when group decision-making approaches are used. "Sharing the agenda" in this respect can function as a most effective management tool.

Therefore, group participation in the establishment of classroom rules may be an asset to the setting of classroom behavior standards. Before inviting students into the process, however, it is imperative that the educator formulate and clearly spell out the behavioral expectations for the class. Students may then extrapolate to determine specific behaviors which may contribute to the achievement of the expectations by identifying those behaviors that are plainly unacceptable in the learning environment. Thus, rules are born.

What if learners are too immature or unskilled to participate in the decision-making process? Or, what if the teacher is not comfortable with student participation in rule setting? Some brief guidelines that follow may be helpful in establishing classroom rules.

1. Once behavioral expectations have been communicated, make certain that students understand these ideas in concrete, specific terms. Avoid statements such as "I expect you to act your age." Some students have a very immature notion of how a child is to act at a certain age.
2. Keep the rules reasonable but firm.
3. Keep the rules brief. The fewer rules there are, the easier it will be for students to remember them.
4. Recognize and thank students who model appropriate behavior. This should be done as soon as possible to observably demonstrate to students the correct behaviors and the reward of praise for proper compliance.

The analysis of a typical classroom expectation and accompanying rule illustrates some key factors. An elementary specialist has set the expectation that all students will respect each other in the class. Next, the specialist invited the c hildren to give examples

46

of how they could act and treat others in the classroom
to show respect by asking, "What are some of the things
we can do to keep respect in our music class?" The
children respond by developing the classroom rules pertaining to the expectation: "be polite," "don't hurt
anyone," "raise your hand when you have something to
say," "take turns on the instruments," and "don't cut
in line." The elementary specialist and students then
jointly identify the most important behaviors that will
help insure that a respectful climate prevails.
Through this process the idea of being respectful is
crystallized.

The rule-setting process gives students not only a
more accurate understanding of the rule but also helps
them to realize why such rules are necessary. To illustrate, consider the rule of sitting in your assigned
seat. Observation of that rule prevents many undesirable behaviors such as arguing over seats, hopping from
seat to seat, mad scrambles to certain seats, or the
formation of chatty cliques. Children realize that for
safety and instructional reasons we must have rules.
These procedures are necessary and, admittingly, time
consuming. But they are cost efficient as the school
year continues.

Some teachers mistakenly make the assumption that
all students do, in fact, know what is expected of them
in their classroom behavior. This is a faulty expectation for two reasons. First, most children have more
than one teacher; thus, they have multiple expectations
to deal with throughout the day. Second, students do
not know the specific limits until they are communicated, demonstrated or tested. Fortunately, all teachers are in a powerful position to eliminate a great
amount of "testing the limits" if they establish and
express their behavioral expectations.

In summary, the establishment and conveyance of
the expected behaviors within music classrooms is an
essential ingredient in the prevention of conflict
within the classroom. Once educators are aware of their
attitudinal disposition toward students they can understand their managerial strategies and expectations more
clearly. Strong, high expectations need to be understood by students. Some music educators may wish to
have students partake in the rule-setting process.
Whether or not students participate in the decision

making, classroom rules which set limits to behavior must be formulated and also understood by all learners.

Planning Teacher Behavioral Expectations and Standards

Knowing that music educators are the target audience of this book, I take a risk in saying that many music teachers are the cause of their discipline problems. Unwittingly, of course, they directly or indirectly prevent learning. It is obvious when a teacher neglects disciplinary measures. Other causes are more subtle, such as a delay of discipline or an inappropriate intervention strategy in the handling of classroom conflict. Other mismanagement of classroom events may compound classroom problems. But sometimes teachers do not understand what students expect of them. They may cause special discipline problems.

While teachers have learning and behavioral expectations of students, the students have role expectations of their instructional and classroom manager. Expectancy theory, then, is a two-way construct.

What is to be expected of music educators? Within the field of management, three basic role families have been classified for study. They are interpersonal, informational and decisional. Perhaps the most obvious role expectancy of a teacher is that of the informational type. Students clearly expect the music educator to teach. But under the category of interpersonal role expectations come responsibilities to manage as a figurehead (endowed with formal authority) and as a leader (entrusted to guide and motivate). In short, . students expect the music educator to be the authority leader and manager of their learning and behaviors.

When teachers fail to live up to their students' expectations their authority is not credible. A teacher may back down under stress. A teacher may become lazy in the task of instructional planning. A few teachers may not even care about their students' behaviors. In all of these instances, there follows a breakdown of credibility in the teacher-manager. When the educator fails to appear as a competent manager, the appropriate behavioral responses from students do not occur within the classroom. The quality of instruction is consequently impaired.

What behavior or attributes contribute to teacher credibility? In addition to demonstrated competence as a musician, credibility is often acquired through teacher presence. By projecting the image of a capable manager, a person helps create teacher presence. There are a number of elements to teacher presence. Each is worthy of study.

One simple aspect of teacher presence is that of dress. How many teachers appear professional in their attire and grooming? Because students meet their teachers visually before aurally, a first impression is formed. That first impression (and sometimes long-lasting impression) may assist in the establishment of suitable respect and rapport during the initial encounter with students as well as on a daily basis. Although some may argue that one's apparel is a superficial element to credibility, it remains to be a significant one. Annually millions of dollars are spent by people who attempt to create a success image by dress. What is suggested here is for the educator to create a professional image through personal appearance.

It seems that arts educators often receive their share of criticism for their extreme styles of dress. As far as the classroom is concerned, sportswear and formal wear have no place. What the music educator wears in the classroom should be a statement of what type of business is transacted in that room. Teachers are not employed to babysit nor entertain students. Thus, the business of education should be reflected in the educator's attire. This is one way in which the teacher may meet the role expectations of students.

Decisional role expectations are also a natural adjunct to teaching duties. These expectations are elements of teacher presence as well. Because music educators must "take charge," beyond the visual aspect of the manager, an aural element of managerial behavior is to be secured. The most frequently used stimuli in the classroom, the speaking voice, may lend credence to decisional role expectations. All communication, whether positive or negative, is to be sincerely and firmly directed to students. It should sound decisive, i.e. coming from the decision maker in the classroom. A beginning teacher may wish to rehearse communication of directions, reproach or approvals. Tape recording and analyzing the speaking voice may provide a data base for assessing this facet of teacher credibility.

Students have little respect for whimsical, insecure or garbled directions. The affective component to the speaking voice should contribute to a businesslike air. This will insure that instructions are followed without delay or confusion. Communication from the decision maker in the classroom is then transmitted in a credible, pleasant manner.

Another credibility element which may meet students' expectations is that of appropriate language. It is not urgent to speak the vernacular lingo of the particular age group as it is to be sure that students, especially young learners, have a working knowledge of the vocabulary words that are used within the age group. Selection and usage of words in a most propitious manner may contribute to the comprehension of and adherence to directives. To illustrate, "insubordination will not be tolerated on these premises" may not mean very much to a six-year-old child.

In addition to word usage, the effectiveness of vocal communication can also be seasoned by vocal inflection, dynamics and tempo elements of the message. Music educators may wish to tape record their voices as they practice verbal instructions. Depending upon the age and nature of the students, changes in the volume, pitch or speed of the message may drastically alter its import. To be effective, however, these variations in expression require practice and planning.

Finally, nonverbal communication may also contribute to credibility of the educator. As the saying goes, actions do speak louder than words as far as nonverbal behaviors are concerned. Before a mirror, the music teacher may rehearse facial expressions, gestures, postures and movements. It would also be beneficial to arrange for a feedback check to verify whether the intended nonverbal message is actually perceived by the viewer with accuracy.

Music educators should be aware of the role expectations that students have for their instructors. They contribute to their credibility. It behooves educators to examine their appearance and behaviors to identify if these elements of teacher presence contribute to or conflict with the expectations. Such an investigation may provide useful insights into the task of classroom management.

Most educators subscribe to the importance of planning instruction well and thereby fulfill the informational expectancies of teachers. However, some educators may have overlooked the interpersonal and decisional role expectations. A close examination of verbal and nonverbal behaviors may reveal supporting or contradictory evidence. Failing to meet students' expectations may cause subtle conflict in the classroom. The direct ramifications of these failures will most assuredly manifest themselves in some form of instructional or management difficulties.

Matching Philosophy and Practice of Managerial Style

Most music educators are satisfied with their instructional and classroom management style if their approaches work effectively and if their strategies actualize what they believe about students.

A philosophical base for educational management is a necessary ingredient in the formation of management plans. Teachers need to think through their personal beliefs and attitudes toward learning and learners. They must formulate a commitment toward what they believe is important in the education of youngsters. Among these statements of belief priorities can then be ranked. Their practices, finally, may stem from the philosophy.

When teachers are dissatisfied with their management skills it is often due to the ineffectiveness of the strategies. The strategies may be founded upon little or no philosophical foundation. The strategies may or may not represent the teacher's philosophical orientation. It is recommended that congruency be achieved with one's philosophy and management practices. There will exist, then, a framework from which management strategies can be formulated with rationality and consistency.

Therefore, the educators need to analyze carefully whether their music education philosophy is actually in practice throughout their management strategies. If not, adjustment may be forthcoming.

Summary

In this chapter, planning for instructional and behavioral objectives has been analyzed through a number of learning and classroom considerations. In order to assure effective instruction and on-task behaviors, the preparation of instructional plans, the physical accommodations in the environment and the organizational measures need to be examined.

Expectancy theory brings to surface that music educators and students both have expectations of one another. The setting of high, strong and clear expectations assists in establishing the appropriate instructional and behavioral levels of classroom interaction. It was noted that educators who ignore or violate decisional and interpersonal role expectations oftentimes have conflict in their classrooms.

Finally, the acquisition of a match between one's philosophy of music education and one's classroom management practices was suggested. When such congruency exists, an educator may align individual strategies with the philosophical orientation. Whether a music educator leans toward the Theory X or Theory Y disposition, approaches toward classroom events can be executed in a more consistent fashion. The music educator is able to experience satisfaction with managerial approaches because they will represent educational beliefs.

Chapter 3

Questions

1. Through six areas of planning a music educator may prevent problems of an instructional and behavioral nature. List these areas and give a practical exemplar of each.

2. What is the value of thorough and alternate planning, sequencing, pacing, motivating materials and providing aesthetic-laden experiences in music education?

3. What aspects of the physical structure of the classroom can be modified to shape a better learning environment?

4. How can seating arrangements affect student interaction?

5. What type of information about special students should be conveyed to (or investigated by) new teachers to better facilitate an effective music program?

6. What is your perception of the role of parents in classroom management?

7. Since some students perpetually "test" new teachers, why should the teacher make certain to express behavioral expectations and set classroom rules?

8. Formulate five classroom rules. Check them for reasonableness, brevity and clarity.

9. Share your thoughts concerning the educators's responsibility towards the profession of teaching in meeting the role expectancies of students. Include any factors which may assist in the establishment of credibility in the classroom manager. How many of these components can be recognized and refined by the educator prior to the first day of school?

10. On the following continuum place a check to indicate where your beliefs and attitudes lie concerning the education of youngsters.

Theory X	Theory Y
Educator	Educator

11. Place a circle on the continuum above to reflect where your observable management practices lie.

12. In teaching, what concerns you most--the lesson or the behaviors of the students? Where do you spend more time in typical classes--attending to instruction or controlling behaviors?

13. How do your present management practices develop your personal beliefs about students and learning?

14. Utilizing the various aspects of planning effective music lessons, construct:

    a. a lesson plan which provides for a logical sequence of instructional activities for a thirty-minute general music class for elementary age learners, or
    b. a rehearsal period which captivates, motivates and sustains on-task behavior while building momentum and performance skills throughout a forty-minute rehearsal block.

References

DeBruyn, Robert L. "Be nice . . . be mean . . . get rid of them," The master teacher, (Dec. 1, 1980), Vol. 11, No. 12.

DeBruyn, Robert L. "Tailored for your lesson," The master teacher, (Dec. 29, 1980), Vol. 11, No. 6.

Fiedler, Fred E. and Chemers, Mortin M. Leadership and effective management. Glenview, IL: Scott, Foresman and Co., 1974.

Frost, Taggart. Lecture on managerial concepts, University of Northern Iowa, November, 1980.

Hurt, H. Thomas, Scott, Michael D. and McCroskey, James C. Communication in the classroom. Reading, MA: Addison-Wesley Co., 1978.

Kindsvatter, Richard and Levine, Mary Ann. "The myths of discipline," Phi Delta Kappan, 1981, 61.

Leonhard, Charles and House, Robert. Foundations and principles of music education. New York: McGraw-Hill, Inc., 1972.

Merrion, Margaret Dee. "Guidelines for classroom management for the beginning music educator," Music educators journal, (Feb., 1980), Vol. 66, No. 6.

Merrion, Margaret Dee. "Understanding managerial concepts in classroom management strategies," The national association of laboratory schools journal, (Fall, 1981).

Mintzberg, Henry. The nature of managerial work. New York: Harper and Row, 1973.

Peckenpaugh, Adah. "The teacher and preventive discipline," Discipline in the classroom. Washington, D.C.: National Education Association, 1974.

Small, Ann R. "Pace yourself," Music educators journal, (May, 1979), Vol. 65, No. 9.

Chapter 4

The Effective Music Educator in Action

When I asked a group of adults to recount stories of their most memorable music teachers, their responses were sparse. Repeatedly similar responses to this question have indicated that among the groups of adults to which this question has been posed, very few have had fond memories of exciting school music teachers. Perhaps my informal survey sample is a bit skewed in the number of negative or indifferent responses to the question. Nonetheless, very few persons have encountered effective music teachers in their formal schooling experiences. Why is there a paucity of master-model teachers of music?

Perhaps the scarcity of outstanding music educators may be explained in part due to the conservatory approach to teacher training. When a school of music is primarily concerned with the performance, applied and recital dimensions of the music education degree, there is less commitment, time and emphasis to bring about teaching competencies. Traditionally, music educators are prepared for their careers in what is viewed as two discrete areas--the music training and the professional sequence of education courses. Somewhere in between lie a few methods courses.

Conservatories train musicians and music teachers to be musicians. But they must also be educators if their careers are in school music. There is a need to prepare quality music educators who are competent performers as well as competent teachers. Therefore, with reference to the unique concerns of music education, characteristics of effective educators as perceived by students, administrators and researchers warrant examination. Presented in this chapter are such attributes.

These characteristics are referenced by research findings, learning theory and educational psychology theories. They include the following attributes:

1. being consistent
2. being fair
3. being trusting and respectful
4. being a good listener
5. being credible

6. maintaining a supportive, positive attitude
7. motivating students energetically
8. being firm yet friendly

Each of these teaching behaviors has specific ramifications for the music educator. The analysis for
each shall provide definitions and practical applications within the music classroom.

At the outset, two key questions deserve attention:
For what reason does the educator develop these particular characteristics? How does the educator develop
these particular characteristics? If the educator can
recognize the meaningfulness and usefulness of the
teaching behavior, perhaps the characteristic may be
perceived as desirable within one's teaching style.
What remains, then, is to investigate how one can acquire and develop the particular behaviors.

Being Consistent

Teachers may build structure into their classrooms
by organizing routines and establishing procedures of
operation. Having consistent procedures gives stability
and organization to the classroom climate--a psychological necessity for all learners. Having consistent procedures does not necessarily imply a regime of dull, re-
strictive and repetitious activities. Within the teaching and learning structure there is always room for
flexibility and creativity. In fact, flexibility is
necessary. However, the structure must exist within the
classroom as a modus operandi in order to standardize
routines and to predict behavioral events.

For example, if a classroom rule is to be perceived
as a required behavior, it must be enforced and observed
from day to day and from student to student with a systematic approach. An expected code of behavior will be
appropriate from September through June for each student
within the class. From educational psychology research
we know that a regular reinforcement schedule (positive
or negative) will serve to increase or extinguish behaviors most efficiently. Thus, consistency in one's
management approach can truly modify student behavior.

In the music class a teacher may have the rule
which forbids talking during sectional rehearsal.
Allowing one student to talk would be license for others

to abuse the rule even if the circumstances seem extenuating to the student. Consistency in enforcing classroom rules and procedures firmly and clearly establishes order within the learning environment.

An instructional consistency may be seen in the sequence of learning events such as warmups, scales or other exercises at the opening of the rehearsal. The established routine gives students a psychological comfort in knowing how to behave and what is expected of them. Instructional consistency establishes an expectancy of behavioral events as well.

Being Fair

It is difficult to discuss fairness without some reference to consistency. A fair teacher is consistent. Classroom and instructional treatment is carried out without serious deviation from person to person or situation to situation. Fairness is a characteristic of teachers that is perceived as most essential to the learning environment, particularly by junior high students. Ranking above a competent or an interesting instructor, students value a fair teacher.

Like consistency, fairness builds structure. More importantly, fairness builds integral, interpersonal working relationships with students that yield trust. Students have firm expectations of the interpersonal roles of their teachers. When students observe a teacher manage classroom conflict they form an expectation that future conflict will be handled on a similar basis. In fact, some students are intently concerned that they receive the exact reward or punishment as fellow classmates. Understandably, then, teachers must continually strive to be fair in their intervention strategies.

The task of maintaining a fair climate within the classroom is a most challenging endeavor for the educator. Four situational factors may vary. (1) Students are not identical. (2) Incidents of conflict are rarely the same. (3) Infringement upon certain rules at certain times may differ according to the student's "history" of classroom behavior. (4) Teachers know that some intervention strategies are more effective with some students than with others. Each instance of conflict may not be resolved with the identical approach. However, each incident can be dealt with fairly.

Returning to the rule forbidding talking during sectionals, suppose one student is chatting quietly about a college acceptance letter. Later during another sectional, another student loudly talks and causes the entire alto section to laugh. Despite the different circumstances, both students have broken the classroom rule. Both students must be reprimanded for the rule to abide.

It might be mentioned at this point that because of the great concern for fairness among pupils, it is suggested that whenever possible it is advisable to discipline students privately. The reason is thus: when disciplining, it is the specific behavior which needs attention, not the student. Some students may actually enjoy the class attention during public disciplinary action. Private disciplining may further help to eliminate opportunities for students to compare or complain about discrepancies in teacher behavior. These concerns are side issues and they thwart the corrective measures. Once again, whether privately or publicly, students have expectations that the teacher will manage the classroom in a fair manner.

Being Trusting and Respectful

The old adage that warns one to earn respect before expecting it has significant implications for educators. The teacher's respect for students may serve as an excellent behavioral model. Students are able to learn, first hand, that if they wish to be treated properly, they need to treat others accordingly. The Golden Rule is one expectation which illustrates mutual respect in action.

Earlier it was suggested that a teacher's consistency and fairness directly contribute to the quality of relationships with students. These attributes are also strong indicators of respect. A classroom with a healthy rapport has strands of respect, fairness and consistency woven into the climate fabric. Such a special atmosphere is created around trusting student and teacher relationships. For example, the music educator may express to the students, "I trust (expect) that you will behave in a certain way." This is to say, "I believe in you."

A trusting rapport with students contributes to

an atmosphere that is less conducive to turmoil, surprise and disruption because the teacher is perceived as a structured, organized, consistent and fair manager. The students, in return, are expected to fulfill their responsibility to learn and to act appropriately within the classroom.

It seems as though there may be some unique strategies a music educator may employ to secure and promote respect within the classroom. Because music educators frequently have contact with a greater number of students and in a different capacity than the traditional classroom interaction, special effort must be made to learn each student's name in all performing groups, in all levels of general music classes or in other nonperforming classes. Without some personal identity within the classroom, the student is likely to feel little accountability for learnings or behavioral expectancies having a low profile. Further, the performance level may not be optimal should a student feel e pluribus unum.

There are other reasons why music educators need to know students' names. These will be more fully addressed in later discussions. But for present purposes, keep mindful that students have a desire to be recognized as individuals even within a large group. By knowing each student's name, the teacher has established one form of respectful attention to that individual.

Being a Good Listener

One of the most effective ways to nurture mutual trust and respect is to insure that two-way communication lines are always operant within the classroom. Because the majority of music teaching is teacher-directed instruction, music educators may wish to frequently check themselves on this trait. If the teacher transmits all of the instructional information and students absorb accordingly, the one-way learning is limited to the insight of one person in that learning environment. Without open two-way communication, it is difficult to assess what exactly has been learned and how it has been learned. Students need to express themselves and demonstrate the reconstructed learning. Teachers must develop astute listening skills.

When a teacher demonstrates good listening skills, that teacher is perceived as an understanding adult. Marshall defines emphatic understanding as the trait of "listening sensitively and accurately to another with the goal of perceiving through the eyes of others and understanding from his frame of reference" (p. 22). Without listening to student views and ideas, teachers have little understanding beyond their own.

This important characteristic of effective class-room teachers has merit when the instructional manager is able to sense the affective climate and make adjust-ment accordingly. It requires skillful listening plus understanding. If students, for example, do not enjoy the selected repertory, or if students have lost inter-est at the outset of a listening lesson, the skilled listener will modify the learning situation to avert possible classroom conflict. Perhaps the planned reper-tory can be introduced at a later date; the attentive listening lesson should incorporate charts or visual aids to sustain an active listening participation. Planning, the necessary preparation for the instruction-al or behavioral events, was mentioned in the previous chapter. However, unplanned classroom events require careful listening and interpretation.

Students grow in respect for individuals who under-stand and listen to them verbally and nonverbally. For it is not only a situation of "hearing students out," but it is also that of understanding "where they come from." The context of comments, in addition to the pur-pose of and circumstances in which the communication is made, requires careful analysis.

Therefore, in the interests of effective classroom management, the music educator must begin listening for things beyond intonation and rhythmic accuracy. Inves-tigating how students feel about the repertory studied or the activities of the program will provide some understanding of student affective levels. Teachers may then know the "total" music interests of their stu-dents, such as choir membership, private lesson study, local band membership, or even their favorite Top 40 hit. All of this information can help the music educa-tor direct the education of students with more refer-ence.

Being Credible

As soon as students perceive the instructional and management competencies of the music educator, the teacher is recognized as credible. The most talented and gifted performer will be ridiculed and largely disrespected if the behavioral management role is not handled effectively.

When music educators are hired, an assumption and expectation is made that graduates of accredited, teacher preparation institutions will be competent in the instructional phases of preparing and delivering lessons, in understanding the scope and sequence of learning events, and in the musical competencies for the partiular specialization. Inexperienced teachers, indeed, may not be strong in each of these areas. Yet it is of utmost importance for the new faculty member to come to the teaching situation with a degree of self-assurance. Elan is necessary to carry out the instructional and classroom duties. Teachers need to know their music, the learning processes and the strategies necessary to bring about music education. They may need to convince themselves and others that they are capable in each area, i.e. credible teachers.

Unfortunately, the expectancy that the bachelor's degree or state certification will insure competency in these important areas is a false one. Many teachers, particularly new members to the profession, lack self-assurance. When their musical skills are weak, they falter in their students' presence. Weak teachers lose respect and trust. Meanwhile, students may take advantage of the teacher's insecurity. The lack of respect and trust may permeate the classroom climate resulting in classroom conflict.

Specifically, what can music educators do to develop credibility? First and foremost, they must know their music. They must prepare for their teaching. Second, they need to know their students as quickly as possible. Along with efforts to learn names, they must treat students fairly in a consistent fashion, expecting and requiring reciprocal interaction throughout the classroom. The competent teacher is well on the road to credibility by establishing expectancies, rapport and interest in the learners. Third, music educators must have effective instructional and classroom management

approaches. Musical competencies, academic preparation
and skills in management practices provide an instructor
with tools to build a credible profile. They also provide the music educator with confidence to be effective
in the classroom.

Maintaining a Supportive, Positive Attitude

When students contribute to a stimulating learning
atmosphere, they should be recognized for helping create
a positive environment. Sometimes contributions may
take the form of a simple comment. It may be the way
in which a student participates in band or chorus which
truly enhances the morale in a positive fashion. The
students' contributions should be recognized, rewarded
and, hopefully, modeled.

Teachers may also make contributions. They may
secure and maintain a strong, positive learning climate
through their personal, supportive attitude. With a
positive attitudinal disposition, more emphasis will be
placed upon good things that are occurring in the learning environment. An example of this strategy is when the
director points out to the orchestra how much repertory
has been successfully rehearsed that period. Prime time
may be given to showcase talented learners, appropriate
behavior and positive aspects in the classroom. The
music educator may remark how well the students have
met the behavioral expectations as well.

Very often peer modeling results as students
quickly adapt to the proper way of learning or behaving.
The following hypothetical situation illustrates the
point:

Ms. A remarks, "Randy, I don't like your posture."
Mr. B remarks, "Mandy, super posture! I hear a
difference."

The first comment is, of course, negative. Randy and
other students know that Ms. A does not approve of his
posture. But do they know what the desirable posture
is and why it is desirable? Mandy does. All of the
students, hearing the reinforcing praise, know what the
appropriate posture is and why it is appropriate. Other
students are now able to understand the musical importance of good posture and to model the appropriate posture.

Both comments virtually required the same amount
of teacher energy and time. However, both comments
differed in appeal and effect. If a positive learning
attitude is desired throughout the classroom, a considerable percentage of compliments, acknowledgements,
"thank you's" and positive reinforcement must be inte-
grated within the instructional program.

Aside from the instructional and behavioral bene-
fits of the manager's positive attitude, something very
important is apt to result from a positive disposition.
The educator is able to directly contribute the
learner's self-concept growth as the student becomes
aware of positively reinforced behaviors. Students,
indeed, feel good about themselves as a result of
praise. Finally, the expected learning behaviors are
recognized and modeled--a most valuable classroom experience.

Motivating Students Energetically

In my teaching experiences I have often felt that
students have no time to misbehave! That is, they are
so actively engaged in the learning process that to-
gether we are too intent on the task to bother to de-
viate. Only the teacher can provide this type of im-
petus drive to process the instructional lesson. When
music educators approach the learning process, the
learning environment and the learners with an enthusi-
astic, energetic drive to accomplish their goals, they
often motivate by osmosis. The intensity of their invitation to learn is contageously caught by the students!

At the other extreme, a lack of motivation on the
student's part is sometimes perceived as the root of
many instructional and behavioral problems. A careful
analysis of what motivates children may uncover new
strategies to manage directly the seemingly "unmoti-
vated" or "problem" learner. Something motivates
everyone. The task remains to identify just what that
"something" is for the particular student.

Consider the following junior high choir scenario.
Several of the boys were singing the tenor line in an
octave displacement range and refused to sing it in
their head voices (falsetto). The choir director had
demonstrated the proper vocal production but the boys

labeled the music as "sissy" and "fruity-sounding." The director asked what made the music sound "sissy." One of the boys mimicked in a high, squeaky voice, "all of those high notes." The falsetto voice was not perceived as a legitimate, pleasant tessitura among the boys in the choir. The next day, the director brought in a recording of the Bee Gee's "Stayin' Alive." The director asked the students if they were familiar with the words. Most students began singing along with the recording immediately. Abruptly the needle was lifted, while the students continued to sing momentarily. (In this rock song, of course, only the falsetto vocal technique is used.) The director asked the choir if they thought the Bee Gees were "sissy." "No way!" they answered. The director also asked if anyone recognized the vocal range of the male singers. When they returned to the octavo that called for a falsetto tessitura in the tenor line the director requested that the boys use their "Bee Gee voices." In this case, motivation led to inspiration.

This scenario helps illustrate that the motivation task is not always simple, but it is very worthwhile. Once the music educator is skilled in motivating students to accomplish musically worthwhile goals, the manager has fewer difficulties. For the linkage between what students perceive as desirable and what the music educator wishes to accomplish is made.

When students are energized by their instructor's enthusiasm for music they not only spend more time on-task but they generally have excellent classroom behavior. Specifically, it was noted in a research study that teachers who vary their proximity, vocal inflection, engage in effective eye contact, demonstrate good listening skills and maintain this energetic state have excellent classroom control. Thus, the ability to motivate energetically and maintain students' interest serves the instructional objective with greater time on-task and the classroom management goals with improved behavior.

Being Firm and Friendly

A no-nonsense approach in all transactions with students is desirable in terms of a working rapport. It is not necessary to mimic the antics of a drill sergeant nor is it necessary to become a wishy-washy weakling when dealing with students. A firm but friendly approach in verbal and nonverbal language is most effective. The educator may communicate and act in a no-nonsense manner without losing the integrity of the reprimand nor the relationship with the student.

Students need to understand the seriousness of school business. They must take responsibility for their learning and accept the consequences for misbehavior. Sweet talking, cajoling, ridiculing or embarassing students for any reason has never proven to be effective in the long run. Teachers who employ sarcasm or sugar-coated pleas for behavior management techniques lose respect among students. This is to suggest that the manner in which a message is conveyed to students may determine whether or not it will be followed or understood.

Inadvertently a teacher may clutter a message to students with inappropriate social distance or other nonverbal signals. Being as direct and straight forward as possible helps the clarity of communication. In an adult manner, students must learn to receive reprimand. However, teachers must conduct themselves as adults too. Unless teachers demonstrate the appropriate communication manners, students are apt to out-shout, return cryptic remarks, retort with hidden inuendo or mimic an inappropriate style.

Social distance is one facet of communication used considerably but often it is not utilized effectively. Music educators may wish to employ strategies which help establish direct, straight forward communication in this area. The proximity with which a statement is made often affects its impact. A random comment, "You, in the fourth row, keep quiet," during rehearsal may not be nearly as effective as walking up to and directly confronting the student in the fourth row about the talkativeness.

It is possible to be firm and friendly in other types of communication such as through the teacher's posture, eye contact, gestures and facial expressions. It is interesting to note that many of the nonverbal messages that are sent to students do not always confirm the verbal content of the communication. A careful analysis of communication techniques and styles may yield a more accurate understanding of its impact.

Videotaping a music educator without sound may provide a nonverbal data base for analysis purposes. The music educator may wish to master an array of nonverbal strategies to coincide with a firm, no-nonsense verbal approach for managing students.

Summary

It is obvious that a number of the characteristics of effective teachers are contingent upon and congruent with each other. The development of one trait perhaps creates readiness for the other traits to blossom and coexist. This was demonstrated in the relationship between consistency and fairness with a trusting climate as a result.

Keeping students on-task without losing momentum from the start of a lesson to its finish is no small charge. The physical and psychological energies required to manage instruction and behavior effectively are astronomically demanding. Yet they are cost efficient in that the managerial efforts of this nature insure that the music educator may truly educate. The educator is then able to appreciate the musical growth of students. Teaching and learning become very satisfying and rewarding activities. It seems to me that this is what teaching is all about.

Though master teachers may possess many characteristics that are attributed to effective educators, that does not insure that their classrooms are conflict-free. Inappropriate behavior occurs despite the most meticulous, preventive measures. Because some behaviors are unpredictable, the music educator must have effective intervention strategies to manage situations in which individuals or groups of students behave inappropriately.

The discussion in the following section addresses specific intervention techniques for the individual misbehaving student. Managerial approaches for groups are explored in the section immediately following.

Managing the Inappropriate Behavior of the Individual Student

There are a number of systematic approaches to discipline which are currently employed in classrooms.

67

Two of these approaches, the LEAST Approach and Assertive Discipline, are research based. The LEAST Approach and the Assertive Discipline strategy have been utilized with a degree of success by many educators. While the LEAST Approach has been endorsed by the National Education Association, Assertive Discipline grows out of Assertion Training. National training seminars and local workshops are regularly conducted to promulgate the basic classroom management philosophy and to demonstrate the strategies in action.

The LEAST Approach is a five-step procedure which outlines graduated teacher reactions to student behavior problems. The Assertive approach is based on the premise that the teacher must assert classroom order by enforcing rules or the consequences of ignoring rules. It is disappointing to find that these approaches do not incorporate instructional management as an important determinant of classroom behavior.

Project TEACH is a training course approach to classroom management which uses a variety of learning modes and covers specific verbal skills and techniques to help educators become more effective teachers. Such skills as questioning and paraphrasing techniques, problem-solving skills, counseling techniques and momentum strategies are elements of the training course. PRIDE is another course which utilizes multimedia resources to cover such topics as the analysis of non-verbal communication, behavior modification and further refinement of questioning techniques. Both courses are offered to teachers in twenty states and provinces on a graduate or inservice basis. Project TEACH and PRIDE are combined instructional and classroom management approaches to teacher effectiveness.

NEA has published a <u>Classroom Survival Manual</u> which contains many excellent suggestions for establishing classroom discipline. The National Education Association publication emphasizes the importance of classroom organization, recognizes the teacher as the authority and leader figure, and explores some instructional causes and solutions to discipline problems. The manual stresses the importance of being aware of situations which may precipitate discipline problems. Suggested are specific solutions to such persistent problems as tardiness, disorder in the classroom and disobedient behavior.

Generally, most classroom management approaches use some form of behavior modification. Behavior modification is an attempt to change patterns of practiced behaviors which are inappropriate and unacceptable within the classroom. Behavior modification may have its function also in shaping desirable, appropriate behaviors.

Behavior modification is a widely employed approach to dealing with discipline problems. The approach assumes that student behaviors are simply learned ways of adjusting to the classroom environment. The behaviors are not manifestations of serious emotional disorder. Therefore, if environmental situations and direct consequences of behaviors can change, students may learn appropriate behaviors. Most teachers, consciously or unconsciously, have employed some form of behavior modification within their classrooms.

Through positive behavior modification, desirable behaviors may be strengthened by the teacher, the students or the environment. Undesirable behaviors may be weakened and eventually eliminated. Behavior modification involves the use of learning theory and the principles of conditioning. Seven intervention strategies that the educator may utilize in the process of modifying inappropriate behavior follow:

1. The music educator may alter the conditions which have allowed or suggested the student's undesirable behavior.
   Illustration: It is possible to modify behavior by changing a student's seat.
2. Awarding a positive reward to the student for not engaging in inappropriate behavior is a powerful, positive strategy.
   Illustration: The student with excellent posture may be given an opportunity to perform a solo.
3. The music educator may award a negative reinforcement (punishment) to the student for repeating an undesirable behavior.
   Illustration: A punishment may be administered by keeping a disobedient student after school.
4. Ignoring the student, i.e. granting no reinforcement, may be another powerful technique.
   Illustration: In this strategy, the teacher avoids giving attention to the student who sings off-key purposefully for class attention.

5. To reinforce a behavior which is incompatible with the inappropriate behavior also causes behavior change.
   Illustration: The director may announce, "Your voices sound beautifully when they are singing" (as opposed to when they are talking during rehearsal).
6. The music educator may administer soft repremands only to the misbehaving student.
   Illustration: The teacher may whisper to the disruptive student, "I will see you after class."
7. Contracting a response cost system with the student involving point loss, fines or elimination of privileges frequently modifies behavior in short order.
   Illustration: The teacher "docks" the tardy students the number of minutes which they have missed. The students are required to make up the lost time during lunch or other inconvenient period of time.

There are several operational factors to keep in focus when using behavior modification techniques for intervention strategies. First, a systematic approach to reinforcement with a regular, consistent schedule of rewards or punishments is absolutely essential. Erratic consequences for behavior do not effectively reinforce or extinguish. For example, if a student is contracting a response cost system for not talking in class, it is imperative that the student be monitored at frequent and regular intervals of time. By consistently providing feedback for the desired/undesired behavior the student "learns" most effectively what is appropriate by continually controlling the urge to talk.

Second, the student must find the consequences of the behavior meaningful whether they are rewards or punishments. This appears to be the crux of behavior management. To reward or punish students with a consequence which does not particularly affect them is defeating the purpose of the strategy. It is very useful to identify those rewards which will make the consequence truly worthwhile and effective. Punishments should be perceived as avoidable. To illustrate, some students do not mind staying after school as a punishment. However, if their punishment is to forfeit lunch or recess timethey more immediately feel its impact.

The intent of the strategy is to make it a meaningful intervention. Therefore, it is suggested that the punishment or the reward receive the student's full attention.

Third, the consequence or reinforcement should follow the behavior immediately whenever possible. A time lag may cause serious delay and negate the effectiveness of the intervention. Teachers who wish to modify behavior must do so with appropriate action which attends to the behavior with immediate consequences. A reward or punishment several days after the incident has lost some of its impact.

Fourth, there are many types of reinforcement rewards which may be chosen for particular purposes. Typical reinforcement modes are physical, social, affective or musical. Some students appreciate a handshake; others may prefer a verbal reward in the form of praise. Each student is individual in this respect and the music educator will need to determine the most effective rewards systems for each class member. To illustrate, a number of students at the junior high age level would prefer not to be praised among peers; however they may welcome the approval and verbal praise in a different setting such as at a parent conference.

An important factor often overlooked is the fifth point. The success of behavior modification is dependent upon the clarity with which a student understands the purpose and goal of the modification system. The more aware the student is, the more accountable the student may behave. This responsibility of the behavior modification system lies entirely with the music educator. The teacher needs to help the student understand the objectives for and reasons why the system is operant. An example of this operational step being overlooked is when the music specialist removes the classroom instrument from the student who plays it inappropriately. Rather, the teacher needs to demonstrate how to properly play classroom instruments, explain the function of instrumental accompaniment and remind the student that if the instrument is abused the privilege will be removed. The child then knows the purposes and goals of appropriate behavior.

Finally, though an extrinsic reward system may be employed and small gains may be planned initially, the teacher may gradually move toward the ultimate behavioral goal: self-control. As soon as possible, the music educator may transfer the reward system to an intrinsic one. If the system of behavior modification is articulately managed, the musical and aesthetic rewards can be timely incorporated. The aesthetic reward, an intrinsic one, is a very powerful one too. Since aesthetic ends are our ultimate goals, it seems only reasonable that direction in this effort be made. Strategically, efforts in this direction may be planned as part of the instructional and behavioral plans. Aesthetic responses to music, such as prizing, appreciating and valuing music, can also be transferred to student behavior: prizing, appreciating and valuing their class membership.

There is no doubt about the validity of behavior modification as a management tool. It works. The one disadvantage, however, is that of time. The music educator will need to make the investment of time to plan, diagnose, explain, execute and follow up in the systematic approach. Nonetheless, if the undesirable behavior is of concern, it is worthy of time and attention.

Music teachers, like all teachers, are concerned with instances of conflict in the classroom. Immediately the reaction to conflict may be one of reprimand. Yet behavior modification experts insist that the positive reinforcement of appropriate behavior is significantly more powerful than reprimand. Specifically, the use of praise and approval for desirable behaviors is recommended. The praise intervention strategies are very effective. Modeling, shaping and token reinforcement interventions are additional techniques which emphatically increase appropriate behaviors that the teacher may wish within the classroom. If clear rules and expectations are introduced to the students, it is then necessary to recognize and model examples of those rules and expectations.

The proper management of individual behavior can yield not only a healthy social climate but also a better learning environment. The classroom contains many valuable energies which can be directed in a number of ways. Unless skillful attention is given to the harnessing of these energies, discipline problems may occur as the energies are directed into the wrong channels (Brand). The management task, then, might be conceived as a redirection effort rather than a suppressive or combative approach to conflict in the classroom.

The conflict situation requires introspective analysis by the music educator. Self-examination questions, such as "Was there anything in my planning which may have inadvertently precipitated the conflict?," examining the lesson, rehearsal, sequencing, procedures, pacing, activities, evaluation of environmental factors for their effect upon the problem are further areas which the educator may begin to analyze. The second phase of the investigation may lead to an exploration of possible changes in the teaching strategies, environment, scheduling, or other classroom variables. In this introspective assessment of the situation, the educator is more likely to discover creative, problem-solving solutions to conflict.

Problem-solving of this nature is a subjective process. It is personal assessment. Because the teacher is the adult in the classroom, it is hoped that a thorough analysis of the problem will be made. It is further hoped that the manager will possess the insight, sensitivity and courage to modify what needs alteration.

Finally, should teachers wish to view themselves as others experience their unique instructional and classroom management style, they may arrange for a videotaping of a lesson. Perhaps the tape may reveal some relationship between teaching style, instructional strategies, management approaches and responding behaviors among pupils. It may be helpful to invite a feedback person who would provide additional observation and reactions. The outside person may more objectively provide feedback. The music educator may then reconcile external observations and internal assessment of teaching behaviors and student behaviors.

Sona Nocera's Reaching the Special Learner Through Music addresses special strategies the music educator may utilize in coping with mainstreamed students. Though her recommendations are catalogued according to disabilities, the majority of her suggested instructional techniques are applicable to any group of learners. Additional ideas for dealing with misbehavior which may interfere with learning may be found in this fine publication.

Managing Inappropriate Behaviors of Groups

Class discipline problems differ from individual discipline problems in two ways. First, when the entire class is out of order the managerial weakness is frequently instructional in cause. Second, the choice of intervention strategy that is suitable for group discipline problems often differs from strategies appropriate for an individual. With little exception, individual management strategies which were disclosed in the preceding section are not applicable to group discipline situations. Clearly, however, "group punishment" techniques are not effective nor fair strategies to employ. Often it is the case that the undesirable side effect of group punishment precipitates more conflict than originally present!

What is necessary in large group instruction is an understanding of group dynamics and group processing skills. Since music educators typically encounter groups of students in medium to large composition, it would be to their managerial advantage to understand groups well. To grasp an understanding of some of the characteristics of groups and conflict within groups, a hypothetical case is proposed for analysis.

    Place: Unowhere Junior High School
    Class: General Music
    Time: November
    Instructor: Miss Knowitall

A unit in Medieval music has been presented to junior high general music students. Miss Knowitall has complained to the principal, Mr. Takecharge, that the students are not completing assignments, nor are they participating in the activities. Further, the entire class has failed the quiz. During the third week into the unit, Miss Knowitall asked for discussion on the homework assignment. No students volunteered to discuss. She was furious and lost her temper with the silent class, threatening that they will all be receiving failure warnings as Mr. Takecharge suggested. She returned the quiz papers. The students were tense and discouraged. At lunch time a conversation between two rather solid students went something like this:

"How'd you do on the quiz?"

"Aced it, what do'ya think?"

"Ha! You liar. Hey, I hate that class. I'm in trouble if she sends a failure warning home."

"Yea, me too. But what can we do? I don't even know what she's talking about in there--with that stupid middlevil music or whatever it is! Half the time I don't know what we're doing. It's so boring. And I don't want to ask any questions. Why do we have to study that stuff anyway?"

"I don't know. And today she was asking about stuff that wasn't in chapter three."

"We didn't have to read chapter three."

"Yes, we did. Tnat was our homework."

"No, it wasn't. She told us to finish reading the other chapter and look over the questions."

"Hey, cool it. Here she comes."

The next day an argument broke out between four students in the general music class. Before Miss Know-itall knew it, twenty students were yelling, slamming around books and chairs. An eraser was thrown across the room, breaking a window. In short, the class was in a chaotic state.

Who or what is to blame for the discipline problems in the case? This example flagrantly illustrates five critical problems within the learning group. All problems, of course, are not chiefly caused by the instructor alone, nor by the students alone. Many problems, however, erupt due to a lack of an understanding of effective group management.

It is possible to identify the signs which foreshadowed trouble prior to the uproar in the class. With those warning signals in mind, compare the following antithesis, i.e. the characteristic dynamics of healthy groups.

1. The task and objectives of the learning are well understood.
   Problem in the case: During the third week,

students did not know much about Medieval
music nor why they were studying it.

2. Clear assignments are communicated to all
   group members.
   Problem in the case: There was some confusion
   as to what precisely was the homework assignment.

3. There is a great deal of discussion amid the
   group.
   Problem in the case: No volunteers came forward to discuss the reading assignment.

4. Within the group there is freedom to express
   feelings.
   Problem in the case: Not only was there a
   shortage of recitation but students were
   afraid to ask questions. The two students
   terminated their gripe session when they saw
   Miss Knowitall coming within earshot distance.

5. A relaxed atmosphere prevails.
   Problem in the case: The students were tense
   and discouraged during class; anxiety after-
   effects were also noted in the lunch discussion.

The class in this hypothetical case was a green-
house for serious discipline problems. Students were
bound to express their tension, confusion and resentment through "acting out" behaviors. Miss Knowitall
could have remedied some of the poor group morale by
improving her communication skills to insure that tasks,
objectives and assignments were better understood by
the students. Knowing the objective of the study, students may interact with the learning material more
meaningfully. They may be more apt to join discussion
and thereby shape a healthier emotional tenor within
the classroom. The students may feel more comfortable,
then, to express their feelings as the communication

lines are two-way. Miss Knowitall may learn about the interests, abilities and attitudes of her students if she were listening. Tests may more accurately be constructed. Lessons may more meaningfully be designed. Learning may more joyfully occur.

The students may remain indifferent or negative towards Medieval music. Many educators have difficulty dealing with students' negative reactions to music or units of study. Certainly each student is entitled to a personal reaction to the experiences. In fact, this is a necessary step in the education of feelings. Teachers may deal with criticism of repertory or units more profitably if they encourage students to support their criticisms with musical reasons. In this example, Miss Knowitall's general music students may react negatively to the Medieval music due to the lack of harmony, the irregularity of the metric flow, or other musical criteria. The analysis of these stylistic criticisms may provide insight to the educator for future selection of units of study. The discussion may also provide a meaningful comparison base as students learn about other types of music and grow more tolerant and understanding in their music preferences.

The same can be true of negative responses to literature studied in performing groups. Often the signals students give directors indicate an over-abundance of one type or style of music, that the music is too easy or difficult, or that the music is over-rehearsed. The observant and understanding teacher will use such feedback to adjust and remedy the learning situation. The group, thereby, functions at a more dynamic level.

Returning to the case study, the junior high general music class needed close attention in terms of group needs and dynamics. Miss Knowitall ignored the fact that the group within her class is a collection of learners with various abilities, interests and needs. Recognizing the dynamic aspects of the group would secure a valuable force in the learning process. Communication linkage between the instructor and members, in addition to communication between members, would greatly increase understanding. Perceived and felt conflict would decrease proportionally.

Fewer inappropriate behaviors are likely to occur if the music educator is knowledgeable and skilled in the area of group dynamics. When inappropriate behavior does occur, a number of techniques may be used to "remanage" or "redirect" group energies. Thermometer plans, subgrouping and contingency management are possible group strategies. The music educator may also wish to refine specific instructional skills which will have a direct, positive influence upon classroom behavior.

Thermometer plans are a type of behavior modification which a music educator may wish to employ in managing group behavior. Avent explains that the thermometer plan may be utilized as a means of motivating greater achievement in music and in classroom behavior. The thermometer indicates the achievement in the form of a chart with feedback levels. Once students jointly determine what constitutes appropriate class conduct they construct classroom rules. If a student violates a rule, penalty points are detracted from the 100% possible score for the day or week.

Avent reports the "efficiency charts, stimulating rivalry with one's personal record, or stimulating interest in group achievement, variously made, have their place in classroom management" (p. 160). It appears that thermometer plans, an effective form of behavior modification for groups, may shape a healthy, competitive climate which promotes excellence in individual achievement and behavior for the welfare of the group. However, it is suggested that teachers diagnose the dynamics of their groups carefully to identify which type of behavioral management would most favorably affect the group. Whereas a number of classes may respond positively to the feedback of the thermometer plans and thereby be challenged to improve behavior, some classes may react negatively, refusing to participate.

One of the facets of group dynamics which can be manipulated by the instructor is that of subgrouping. Grouping techniques can increase the quality and quantity of on-task behaviors. Students, for example, who share common interests are more likely to accomplish instructional goals successfully based upon the commonality of goals. Thus, the technique of using interest grouping as a positive management strategy provides motivation and a cooperative climate for on-task behaviors.

Music educators have always used grouping techniques; however, they may not have utilized them to their fullest extent. To illustrate, consider a typical choral rehearsal with sectional divisions between men and women, high and low voices. As the choir director works with one section, the remaining sections are usually left with nothing to do. Each section could be gainfully profiting from every rehearsal minute as the director perfects difficult areas during sectionals. Sopranos may be asked to hum pianissimo, men may be invited to tap the rhythm of the alto part while the altos are singing. Or perhaps the students could be given a listening question or a theory problem to solve within the music.

Another grouping technique which is not employed extensively is the quartet or ensemble rehearsal. A fifty-member choir turns into several ensembles when the director assigns one or two voices per part. An increase in accountability for independent voice parts and a sharpening of listening skills for balance and blend result. This grouping technique virtually eliminates off-task behaviors as singers are more attentive to their own timbre, accuracy, balance and blend.

Subgrouping can also be profitably employed in the non-performance classes. Very often students are placed in general music classes on a random homeroom basis. These groups are heterogeneous in nature. They include the gifted as well as the disabled learner. Therefore, the general music specialist may wish to group children according to social units. Social grouping is advantageous in that children know with whom they can cooperate. They also may exert positive pressure within their groups to monitor behavior as they cooperatively work on the task.

Two final points about grouping are made by Wrightstone. She warns that teachers should be aware of the purposes of grouping. Second, learners should know the function of their grouping. Haphazard assignments of students into groups may have disasterous results such as mismatched ability levels, personality clashes, and leadership voids or rivalry. Skillful grouping techniques may function as an effective instructional and behavioral tool for management. Group assignments, however, need to be thoughtfully planned.

Group contingency management is a behaviorist technique which may be employed at any grade level. The specialist, for instance, may use contingency management in the following manner. Two or three minutes of "request" time may be reserved in each lesson to reward students for remaining on-task and completing the day's lesson. The request time may be spent singing a favorite song, listening to a selected recording or tape, performing on classroom instruments, playing rhythmic games or creating new handjives to music. The request system outlines similar essentials of behavior modification. The students are awarded self-selected activities during free time which they accrue when they successfully accomplish the learning goals. It is important that the reward activity be chosen by the students, for their selection insures its meaningfulness.

Some educators may question whether contingency management borders bribery. It seems to me that there is no question of ethics in contingency plans. Whereas a bribe is a "pay off" involving a reward for doing something illegal or wrong, there is nothing wrong with students learning and behaving appropriately. The intention here is to shape the appropriate behaviors while accomplishing the instructional goals. Nothing is compromised when desirable classroom events are reinforced. Contingency management is merely the transaction of rewards for desirable learning outcomes or behaviors. Like behavior modification plans for individuals, contingency management may work extremely well for groups.

There are some additional management techniques which have been recently researched that suggest specific instructional strategies are significantly effective in the teaching of groups. In a comprehensive analysis of research on classroom management, Emmer and Evertson made a number of recommendations. Seven teaching behaviors were investigated with efforts to correlate the relationship between teaching behaviors and classroom behaviors. The ingredients of successful lessons were compared with less successful lessons. Ingredients such as task structure, the amount of feedback, the academic interaction or the lesson format were compared to the amount of time students devoted to the learning task. The research uniformally indicated that successful classroom management is positively correlated with a more substantive and structured focus throughout instruction. High rates of academic feedback were

observed throughout successful lessons. Continuous
signals for appropriate behavior were maintained
throughout the instruction.

One of the ways a music educator may wish to provide signals for appropriate behavior is through the
use of praise. Praise is one of the most powerful management techniques available to the teacher. One cannot
underestimate the value of praise as a classroom management tool. When it is sincerely and judiciously appor-
tioned, praise provides positive reinforcement which
identifies the appropriate behavior and models its de-
sirability.

The classroom management research also suggests
that effective managers spend considerable amounts of
time during the first few weeks of school establishing
classroom rules and procedure. Clear academic and behavioral expectations are shared with students at the
outset of the school year. To be sure, research vali-
dates the expectancy theory's place in classroom management strategies.

Finally, whether the music educator is managing
the behaviors of an individual or group, some attention
must be given to the follow-up procedures. Effective
managers not only proactively prepare for instructional
and behavioral outcomes while dealing directly and
promptly with problems as they occur, but they also
follow up to complete the phase of the management task.

The follow-up action may appear in the form of
various procedures. The follow-up may be as simple as
restoration of positive reinforcement with a student
who previously misbehaved. It may be more complex and
detailed depending upon the severity of the problem.
The procedures may include alerting counselors, parents,
administrators or law officers. The choice of the
follow-up action requires skillful decision-making as
to what steps may be the most appropriate course of
action to take. Such factors as the disciplinary code
within the school district, the nature of the disciplinary incident and the community rapport are some
considerations to be made.

Some school districts formulate disciplinary
guidelines with prescribed steps which rigidly outline
the procedures for follow-up options the educator may

consider. Other schools may have little or no structure in this respect. The initial handling of any misbehavior, short of breaking the civil law, rests with
the individual teacher and administrator. For minor
infractions of classroom rules it is generally not necessary to notify other personnel regarding the incident.
However, tracking of misdemeanors (as suggested by the
LEAST approach) may provide accurate recorded data for
further use. Though recording of incidents takes time,
it is quite valuable in verifying a student's history
of behavioral problems.

As soon as feasible, the instructional manager may
wish to restore positive reinforcement with a student
who has been involved in a learning or behavioral problem. Quickly the positive reinforcement begins to shape
the desired behavior. This follow-up action may "clear
the air" of any emotional resentment or residue from an
unpleasant incident. Motivation, to be sure, must resume. Students need to be encouraged to participate
fully and appropriately despite previous problems.

When incidents of serious behavioral disorder
arise, counselors, administrators and parents are likely
to be contacted. Notification generally brings support
in the situation. Keep mindful that parents are powerful partners in the education of their children. They
are fully aware that the number one problem in the
schools is lack of discipline. Further, parents have a
right to know their child's academic and behavioral
status.

Other personnel may provide support of a different
nature once they are advised of an instructional or behavioral difficulty. For example, there are types of
learning and behavioral problems which the music educator cannot solve alone. Take, for instance, the student
who is emotionally disturbed or educationally misplaced.
The teacher may help identify alternate learning environments to meet the needs of the individual member and
the needs of the group at large. Reporting these instructional or behavioral cases to the counselor, special education agency or administrator should be prompt.

When the student's best interest is of prime consideration in all efforts to problem-solve with parents,
counselors and administrators, the problem has a good
chance for being solved with collected expertise from

all parties. Basically, most educators want their students to have a good, successful school experience. But they often cannot do this alone. They need the cooperation from students. They need support from the home. They also may need the expertise of other personnel. If students continually fail to meet the instructional and behavioral expectancies of the class, the educator must seek the advice of the support systems: parents or guardians, the guidance personnel, special education consultants and administrators.

On the other hand, it is advisable for educators to be just as prompt to notify parents, counselors and administrators regarding positive reports. If a student has demonstrated marked improvement, progress should also be shared with parents. Administrators need the positive updating as well, in order to grasp a full, complete profile on students. A follow-up action of this fashion may secure more cooperation from students as they perceive the educator as a fair instructor, reporting positive as well as negative news.

Summary

An effective music educator has a variety of instructional and behavioral management skills. A number of these skills are based upon characteristics with which effective educators manage learners. Music educators may recognize and effectively employ these skills in their programs.

Preventive, proactive and positive management of pupils is superior to shotgun techniques. When music educators have thoughtfully analyzed the purposes and consequences of what they do, they are in a better position to accurately diagnose and administer classroom instruction within a healthy classroom environment. Because there will always be a degree of inappropriate behavior in classrooms, it is helpful to be aware of the many types of intervention strategies which may be utilized to control or modify learner behavior or the learning environment.

The management of individual behavior differs from the management of group behaviors. Since educators work with groups of learners, they need to develop behavior modification skills and group processing skills. This chapter has provided some research-based techniques to incorporate in the management of individual or group behaviors. Once again it was noted that instructional management strategies were found to be the key elements in determining successful lessons and classroom behaviors. Bruce Joyce estimated that ninety percent of discipline problems are instructional problems. It appears that emphasis in instructional preparation, then, should center upon acquiring skills to manage the learning program, taking into account a variety of instructional strategies. Meeting the learning needs of individuals within groups will assuredly eliminate many behavioral problems.

Chapter 4

Questions

1. Recall some of the most effective teachers that you
    have known. Discuss their classroom management
    techniques.

2. From the list of effective teaching characteristics,
    choose three in which you feel fairly strong. Cite
    specific instances which demonstrate how the charac-
    teristic can be translated into everyday events.

3. From the same list, choose three characteristics
    which you would like to strengthen within your
    teaching personality. Brainstorm a number of ways
    in which the characteristics might be developed.

4. Identify two students with which you feel you have
    management problems. Among the strategies explored
    in this chapter, decide which approach may work
    best with each student. Tell why you selected the
    particular approach. If possible, test pilot your
    plan.

5. Construct a set of classroom rules. Tape record
    the announcement of these rules to students.
    Critique your recording for sincerity, clarity and
    firmness. Do the same for your instructional and
    behavioral expectations for chorus, band, orchestra
    or general music. If possible, invite an objective
    auditor to provide feedback on the tape recording.

6. Discuss the advantages of employing grouping techni-
    ques within the music classroom. Discuss the dis-
    advantages. Using a forcefield, decide whether
    grouping can serve your learning objectives in
    effective ways.

7. What is a follow-up action? Why is it necessary?

8. In the following case, diagnose the problem(s) in
    the situation and prescribe a possible follow-up
    action.

        Monica was insolent to the junior high instru-
    mental teacher during rehearsal. Her negative atti-
    tude was obvious one day when she sarcastically

commented, "I don't know why we have to learn this music. What has it got to do with anything?" The music was a challenging, syncopated piece. The band instructor told Monica he would be glad to see her after rehearsal. Monica remained in the band room after rehearsal and verbally attacked the band instructor regarding the low grade she received in band during the last marking period. When the instructor began explaining to Monica that the grade was based upon her growth in technique, her attention and her attitude towards the performing group, Monica became more hostile and walked out of the room.

References

Avent, Joseph Emory. Excellence and errors in classroom management. Knoxville: Joseph E. Avent, Publisher, 1934.

Brand, Sister Helena. "Discipline is . . ." Discipline in the classroom. Washington, D.C.: National Education Association, 1974, pp. 11-15.

Canter, Lee and Canter, Marlene. Assertive discipline. Los Angeles: Canter and Associates Inc., 1976.

A Design for discipline. Washington, D.C.: NEA Instructional and Professional Development, Infopac No. 12, 1978.

Emmer, Edmund T. and Evertson, Carolyn M. "Synthesis of research on classroom management," Educational leadership, 1981, 38, 342-347.

Joyce, Bruce. Lecture notes from Models of Teaching Conference, University of Northern Iowa, October, 1981.

Marshall, Hermine H. Positive discipline and classroom interaction. Springfield, IL: Charles C. Thomas Publisher, 1972.

"Practical Applications of Research," Newsletter of Phi Delta Kappa's Center on Evaluation, Development and Research. June, 1981, Vol. 3, No. 4.

Nocera, Sona D. Reaching the special learner through music. Morristown, NJ: Silver Burdett Co., 1979.

Walker, Hill M. The acting-out child: coping with classroom disruption. Boston: Allyn and Bacon, Inc., 1979.

Wrightstone, J. Wayne. Class organization for instruction. Washington D. C.: National Education Association, 1957.

Chapter 5

A Summary of Management Thoughts:
Good News and Bad News

Success in teaching a music education program requires careful consideration of a number of facets that
are involved in effective management. Understanding
the process of music education enables the teacher to
concommitantly achieve aesthetic ends of instructional
and behavioral purposes. Preventive planning in a
variety of areas can assist in the arrangement of quality learning experiences. During music teaching, instruction and behaviors can be focused through proper
sequencing, pacing, selection of materials and music
planning efforts. Intervention strategies can effectively refocus behaviors. The principles of learning,
theories of expectations, dynamics and processes of
groups plus managerial theories are undergirding foundations upon which specific instructional and behavioral
management practices may be based. Refinement in one's
instructional skills brings improved classroom behaviors. And more effective classroom management directly
improves the quality of learning. Some closing remarks
suggest further managerial considerations.

Studies in child growth and development lend credence to the belief that there are long term effects
from early instructional experiences. Bloom's longitu-
dinal studies identified the crucial development period
to occur during the early years of elementary school experience, specifically grades one, two and three. For
musical development, Fowler suggested that the optimum
growth in musical skills, interests and attitudes occurs
between the ages of three and eleven.

Is there a parallel optimum time to shape student
classroom behaviors? Is there a "crucial development
period" during which positive behavioral growth may
best occur? One psychologist portends that junior and
secondary high school students largely determine their
attitudes towards authority during their classroom experiences with their first six elementary school teachers (Dobson, p. 101).

Perhaps there exists a degree of permanency in
attitude formation during early and intermediate child-
hood education. Certainly Bloom, Fowler and other

experts would concur that quality instructional and behavioral systems must be in effect during the early elementary years to take full advantage of the most opportune time to develop cognitive, affective and psychomotor skill learnings.

Similarly, a well-conceived management system should be in operation during these prime times too. A good classroom management plan should be in effect at all times but particularly during the early elementary years. Experiences in a strong, positive classroom climate which is managed by a competent music educator can help formulate affective responses towards not only music but also towards self-concepts. It seems that early in a child's formal schooling music teachers are in a position to bring about positive, cooperative and healthy attitudes towards authority and responsibility within the classroom.

A case has been built for the necessity of instructional and classroom management in order to affect the quality of music experiences. The unique essence of aesthetic objectives in music education have fortified possibilities for securing and maintaining worthwhile learning experiences which concurrently manage behavior appropriately. Educators are left with the task of conceiving and executing these compatible and reinforcing goals. This "affective connection" is a valuable tool, certainly an item of good news to the music educator.

Discipline is a desirable component in the learning climate. Positive classroom discipline assists students in acquiring self-control and direction in their learning behaviors. To help students become responsible, solid citizens is every teacher's duty. The music educator, too, may partake in this awesome responsibility of education.

Further, discipline is meaningful. No group can process goals without a cooperative and collective effort. Standards for behavior, rules and expectations must operate within all groups. Thus, when teachers collaborate in helping students acquire self-discipline, the management task is a continuous, consistent and developmental process. Music teachers rarely work alone at this task. Rest assured that teachers of other subject areas welcome the commitment and reinforcement of the music personnel in the classroom management task. The truth is that most teachers are vitally concerned about the growth of their students. This comes as a second bit of good news.

Management skills in the realm of student learning and behavior may be sharpened through a number of vehicles. First and foremost, improvement can be possible via an introspective, self-appraisal of one's present skills. If educators retain a mental set of their management abilities which places blame upon students, administration, the lack of learning resources, scheduling or other outside interferences, they are less likely to become fully aware of the positive changes and control which they can exert. On the other hand, perceptive, insightful and sensitive educators can sharpen their skills in the management of learners and learning events. Progress commences with an accurate assessment of the managerial skills that are presently operant.

Other vehicles for sharpening one's managerial skills include inservice training in such areas as discipline approaches (Assertive Discipline, Project TEACH, PRIDE or the LEAST approach), continued course work in behavioral psychology, graduate seminars in music education, managerial courses in business departments and inservice workshops. It is sometimes beneficial to brainstorm along with fellow colleagues to share coping devices, strategies and ideas. The support and opportunity for further skill refinement is truly good news.

What about the unpredictability of student behavior? Yes, this is an item of bad news. Clearly there are circumstances in which music educators have no control. Yet the circumstances may be managed, and refocused once proper instructional and behavioral skills match the situation. The responsibility, then, for sharpening management skills lies within the individual music educator regardless of circumstantial problems. A repertory of skills may successfully prevent, refocus and remedy many unpredictable events.

One aspect in the process of developing managerial skills which may threaten some educators is that of change. An effective educator manages learners and learning environment in a "state of flux." Students,

in the process of education, learn, grow and change
throughout the school year. Situation factors such as
urban or rural locale, student ability, student morale,
scheduling, community and administrational support dictate various management approaches. What works effectively in one town for one music educator may not work
at all for another teacher in different circumstances.
This may occur when a successful teacher from one
school encounters a variety of management problems
given a new environment with differing student popula-
tion. Unfortunately, developing one "management style"
is not always the pass key to success.

The chief elements to incorporate into the development of managerial strategies include perceptivity,
flexibility and diagnostic ability. These managerial
requisites are absolutely essential to develop because
of the great amount of mobility within the teaching profession. It has been estimated that the lifespan of a
teacher at any one position is five years. Therefore,
because teachers will change positions, travel from
school to school or even from town to town, they must be
able to change and diagnose the e necessary adaptations
from one situation to another.

In small communities it is common for the music
educator to teach in two or three different buildings.
Frequently the music person is staffed to teach at a
variety of levels from elementary through secondary
school. An obvious diversification of teaching styles
is necessary as the educator encounters large performing
groups, private lesson instruction, general music and
other non-performance classes. Not only need the music
educator adapt from individual to large group instruction (i.e. learning mode) but from performance to
process-based instruction (i.e. learning style). The
demands in each situation are unique. They mandate distinct instructional and behavioral strategies.

Just as the need exists for specialized medical
care from pediatric through geriatric age groups, there
is a need for special instructional and classroom
approaches for the variety of student age groups. Instructionally, elementary teachers may employ aural
approaches (rote) to the teaching of new songs, while
secondary teachers more successfully may employ visual
approaches (note reading). The same is true of behavioral strategies. The music·educator cannot meet the

various demands of the job without developing diagnostic
skills and adapting to each learning environment. In-
flexibility of managerial approaches may result in bad
news for the teacher and the students.

Finally because music teachers are interested in
nurturing the musical growth for all students, every
instructor needs to be interested in managing classroom
behavior which will foster efficient cognitive, affective and psychomotor skill learnings. Proper behavioral
management will contribute to quality instructional
gains. But only when the music educator attends to both
instructional and behavioral goals can gains be made
efficiently and effectively. Addressing the dual responsibilities can be consistent and congruent with one
another. When both phases of management are attended
simultaneously, more satisfying teaching and effective
learning result.

Conveying clear, firm and high expectations to
students is perhaps the most overlooked step in the management process. Ironically, this step is also one of
the more important stages in the establishment of management strategies. Carefully examining the process of
music education, understanding the purpose and impact
of preventive planning, using group processing skills
effectively, employing behavior modification techniques,
acquiring characteristics of effective educators and
evaluating present skills are but a few of the avenues
educators may pursue in refining managerial skills.

Becoming an excellent music educator is a life-long
process. Experience gradually unfolds the perceptive
teacher with the sensitivity, competencies, knowledge,
skills and attitudes which make for successful teaching.
Consequently, teachers who strive for excellence perpetually assess their skills and inventory their per-
vading attitudes. They grow with new insight and modify
their strategies as hindsight opens channels for new
light and understanding.

Depending upon the educator's disposition toward
hard work (and that's exactly what excellent teaching
is), this may come as good news or bad news. Weak
teachers will not grow to effectively meet this challenge; their students will be the victims of their poor
management. Their students will grow up and join that

large percentage of adults who had difficulty recalling a memorable music teacher.

Excellent teachers will grow to meet the challenges of effective management; their students will be the fortunate recipients of their capable managerial skills.

Unlike the "Lady or the Tiger," you now know what's behind each door. Which door will you choose to open?

Chapter 5

Questions

1. What are some of the situational factors which may influence teachers' management strategies?

2. What is the purpose of analyzing situational factors in the learning or teaching process?

3. Why is it that some music teachers are effective in one teaching position, but ineffective elsewhere?

4. What are some of the tools music educators can use to sharpen their managerial skills?

5. What is the instructional value of excellent behavioral management?

6. To "combat" the bad news (i.e. the demands of music teaching and the overpresence of unpredictable conflict in the classroom), what can the music educator do?

7. On the following page is a list of teacher behaviors which are operant throughout instructional and classroom management operations. Complete the statements by filling in who, how or what after each behavior.

8. On page 95 is a list of characteristics of quality management systems. Assess your present management plan with the criteria listed.

Teacher behaviors in the instructional/classroom management process are:

motivating
guiding
teaching
caring
anticipating
perceiving
handling
preparing
coping
attending
modifying
intervening
planning
grouping
asserting
shaping
praising
correcting
building
relating
sequencing
supporting
monitoring
pacing
painstaking!

Checklist for Quality Management Systems

    usefulness
    efficiency
    effectiveness
    meaningfulness
    systematical
    consistency
    reasonableness
    desirableness
    compatibility
    fairness

References

Bloom, Benjamin S. Stability and change in human characteristics. New York: John Wiley and Sons, 1964.

Dobson, James. Dare to discipline. Wheaton, IL: Tyndale House Publishers, 1970.

Fowler, Charles. "The Tanglewood symposium: music in American society: the changing goals," Music educators journal, (Nov., 1967).

Annex A

Crossword Puzzles

Task: Students should construct crossword puzzles to
demonstrate accurate spelling and vocabulary.
Given the vocabulary words, students will provide numbering and clues on the blank puzzle below. Shade in spaces which are not used.

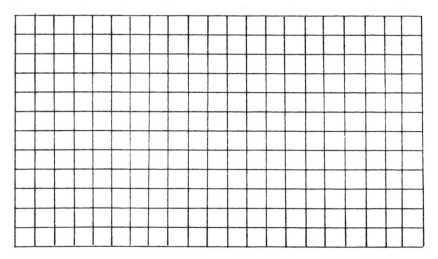

Clues

Across   Down

Notational Error Detection

   In the examples below, there is one rhythmic error
in each line. Circle the error.

   What type of detective are you?

   If you found the error in all three rhythms, you
are a super sleuth! If you found two of the errors,
you are improving. If you found one error, you need a
new magnifying glass! Try harder.

"Nielsen Listening Ratings"

Task: Given cards numbering one through ten, listen
       for specific musical elements such as ostinato,
       syncopation or improvisation. Rate each listen-
       ing composition on the musical criteria. Dis-
       cuss differences in scoring between class mem-
       bers. Compute overall composite rating.

Magic Meter Boxes*

Task: Given the rhythm in the boxes, perform the
rhythms in all directions. Listening to a
rhythm from the magic meter box, decide which
rhythm has been performed.

Duple

Triple

Quadruple

*Students may be given an empty meter box and fill in
their own rhythms.

This activity was learned at a workshop conducted by
Mary E. Hoffman, University of Illinois, Urbana.

101

Concept Wordfinder Review

Clues are given for vocabulary words which have been studied. Write the word next to the clues and find the word in the word puzzle. Words may appear across, down or diagonally.*

Clues

1. All notes are to be sung connected or played smoothly _____

2. Indicates that the tone is to be given added stress and dynamic emphasis _____

3. Abbreviation for go to the beginning of the composition and repeat to the end _____

4. ⌒ indicates _____

5. ‖ :‖ is a _____

6. ($\frac{4}{4}$) ♩♩ indicates a _____

7. How many counts does #6 receive? _____

8. Indicates a gradual decrease in dynamics _____

9. } is a _____ _____ (two words)

10. Abbreviation for gradually getting louder _____

```
T V C E P L E G A T O R I X N O K
M E O T H R E E C L W Q P I R T Y
A C R O R E S T D C A L F I N E P
B K T S A O R F R E P E A T O P R
I N W E S A C C E N T O M N E S O
C R E S E Q U E S L V B P R Z C T
Q U A R T E R R E S T I E V N E R
P I T H Y D E C R E S C E N D O Y
```

*Students may also construct their own wordfinder reviews complete with clues.

Rhythms to Tap

Tap these rhythms forward. Tap them backward.
Write rhythm #2 in $\frac{3}{8}$ time signature.

Initiating Activities

Hangman

Yesterday we learned a new musical term which means the texture contains more than one melody. But the melodies have equal importance. What is this texture called?

As letters to the correct answer are suggested, they are placed in the appropriate spaces. If incorrect letters are suggested, the man is hung by drawing the head, body, arms and legs each time the answer is wrong.

The final Hangman figure appears something like this:

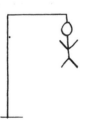

Music Analysis

Using one of the octavos or compositions being re-hearsed, find the answers to these problems.

1. What is the time signature?

2. What kind of note gets one beat?

3. In which measure does your voice/instrument enter?

4. In which measure does the crescendo begin?

5. Where is it possible to take a breath on page five?

6. Which voice/instrument has the melody on the top of page two?

Construction in Rhythm

　　Construct rhythm definitions for new vocabulary words.

$$/ \cup \quad / \cup \quad / \quad \cup \quad / \quad \cup \quad /$$

Example:　duple meter - beats in sets of two.

Spell new music vocabulary words in rhythm.

Example:　duple:　de cr es ce nd o

　　　　　　triple:　tri ple t

Spell new music vocabulary terms with accompanying characteristics.

Example:　legato

　　　　　s-t-a-c-c-a-t-o

107

Name This Tune

Can you tell what tune is written here?

Can you tell what tune has this rhythm?

Index